THE ULTIMATE GUIDE TO LESSON PLANNING

This practical guide will help you to plan evidence-informed, innovative lessons that can be adapted to meet your individual student's needs.

Modelled on a typical lesson plan, the book covers all aspects of planning such as learning aims, starting a lesson, resources and activities, embedding skills, and assessment. Each chapter features a wide range of activities and strategies that can be used every day and easily adapted for different learners. The chapters also explore what to do when lessons don't go to plan and how to use technology effectively to support learning. Throughout there are nuggets of useful theory to help you reflect not only on what works in the classroom but why.

Written by an expert author team and linked to the early career framework, this is essential reading for all trainee and early career teachers across a wide range of educational settings.

Carol Thompson is a senior lecturer and researcher at the University of Bedfordshire. She has over 30 years' teaching experience and more than 20 years working with trainee teachers and mentors. Passionate about sharing her experience, Carol has authored several books aimed at supporting teacher education, including *The Trainee Teacher's Handbook*, *Learning Theories for Everyday Teaching*, *Being a Teacher*, *Reflective Practice for Professional Development* **and** *The Magic of Mentoring*.

Lydia Spenceley has recently retired as a teacher educator but continues her work in education through consultancy and writing. She has worked in various education settings specialising in post-compulsory education and has a special interest in inclusion and special needs education. Lydia is the author of *Learning Theories for Everyday Teaching* and *Inclusion in Further Education*.

Mark Tinney is a teacher educator in one of the UK's largest FE Colleges. Mark has come to FE after several years teaching in secondary and middle school, including running a Montessori middle school programme in upstate New York and teaching high school and GSCE maths and A-level history and sociology. Mark specialises in the use of technology in the classroom and has been training new and experienced teachers to use technology effectively for nearly 20 years.

Elaine Battams, after a career in Early Years, moved into Teacher Education and is now based at Barnfield College in Luton. She is an advanced practitioner supporting others in all things teaching, learning and assessment. A firm believer in reflective practice and self-development, Elaine was one of the first cohort in the country to achieve Advanced Teacher Status (ATS) and CTeach with the Education and Training Foundation.

Ann Solomon is a lecturer on teacher education programmes at Oaklands College St Albans. She has a background in health and education. She has over 20 years' experience in education at various levels including primary, further and higher education. Ann has a special interest in mentoring teachers at all levels of their teaching career.

THE ULTIMATE GUIDE TO LESSON PLANNING

Practical Planning for Everyday Teaching

Carol Thompson, Lydia Spenceley,
Mark Tinney, Elaine Battams and
Ann Solomon

Routledge
Taylor & Francis Group

LONDON AND NEW YORK

Designed cover image: © Getty Images

First published 2024
by Routledge
4 Park Square, Milton Park, Abingdon, Oxon OX14 4RN

and by Routledge
605 Third Avenue, New York, NY 10158

Routledge is an imprint of the Taylor & Francis Group, an informa business

British Library Cataloguing-in-Publication Data
A catalogue record for this book is available from the British Library

ISBN: 9781032473901 (hbk)
ISBN: 9781032473895 (pbk)
ISBN: 9781003385905 (ebk)

DOI: 10.4324/9781003385905

Typeset in Interstate
by Newgen Publishing UK

For Oscar and Iniko - Gone but always with us.

CONTENTS

FIGURES

TABLES

Introduction

You're free next period aren't you?

(Silence)

The Psychology teacher's off sick and I need someone to cover her class ... I know it's not your subject, but all the notes are on the system, you'll be fine. Thanks!

(A wave and a smile. Stage exit left)

Does this seem like a familiar tale? We have probably all been caught out by this type of thing in the past, trying to help out by 'covering' for an absent colleague with the promise of a lesson plan and resources all being in place. Then finding that the lesson plan was pretty much non-existent, and the resources consisted of a single handout. If you have, you probably also remember the sinking feeling of standing in front of a class without any idea what to do and having to 'wing it', knowing all along that the lesson would be nothing short of a disaster. It isn't an experience anyone wants to repeat. But what if, when you logged onto the intranet you found a detailed lesson plan, lots of activities and resources already set up? You might then feel that you could teach the lesson after all. Wouldn't that be a much more positive experience?

The importance of lesson planning is something which cannot be overestimated – not just when you are called on to cover a lesson at short notice. It is a fundamental part of teaching practice, and it makes our own day-to-day lives much easier in so many ways. Knowing you are well prepared gives you confidence, removes the pressure of having to think on your feet and generates a sense of calm. Who doesn't want that? After all, it's hard enough being a teacher without any added stress, so anything that we can do to relieve some of this pressure is a bonus – a well-prepared lesson is one of those things. Yes, it takes careful thought and time in the first instance and yes, you do need to evaluate and adapt each time you re-teach a lesson, but, if executed well, a strong lesson plan is something you can return to time and time again. You won't be able to use it exactly as it is, and having reflected after the lesson you will almost certainly want to make some tweaks. This is a good thing – refreshing, rather than recreating means that you have a solid foundation on which to build. In addition, you have the added bonus of being able to evaluate what went well and what could have been better and can create an even better lesson by acting on these reflections.

It's fair to say that, as authors of a book on planning, we are all advocates of the process and there is good reason for this. Our experience as teachers and as teacher

DOI: 10.4324/9781003385905-1

educators, has provided clear evidence that the teachers who are well prepared, are also the teachers who can take a more flexible approach. It may seem counterintuitive, after all, if we plan in great detail surely, we are placing strict controls on our time? At a superficial level, the answer to that question is 'yes' but, when you remember that a plan is just a plan, it is not a diktat or rule of law, then the picture looks a little different. By planning ahead, you are actually giving yourself permission to be spontaneous, to respond to those important 'teachable' moments and to give your learners some power in co-constructing the lesson outcomes. By planning well, you are also giving yourself some thinking time during the lesson, this is an essential component of reflection within the lesson which will allow you to make small but necessary adjustments to ensure that the learning opportunity is optimised.

If you want to be a great teacher, a teacher who has a positive impact, then good planning will become a part of your toolkit. In our experience, great teachers, present new learning in ways which not only engages their learners but also challenges them. And, perhaps more importantly, they are well aware that this doesn't happen by magic. Great teachers spend a considerable amount of time thinking about, and planning, their teaching. But don't just take our word for it, there is much research to support this, and we will be sharing that with you in the chapters which follow this introduction.

A well-planned lesson is one based on principles of knowledge construction and recognises that learning will not happen at the same time, or in the same way for every learner, as such it demonstrates as much understanding of the process of teaching as of the practice. We cannot simply learn the craft of teaching in the form of competences, such as giving a presentation or carrying out an assessment. We also need to be aware of the theory underpinning practice. We need to know how learners learn, how they retain learning and how they can use it in a variety of situations. We also need to consider the social and emotional aspects of learning, things such as motivation, curiosity and self-efficacy, whilst recognising the significant impact our actions as teachers, and our expectations of learners, have on how much they achieve. There is no formula for all of this, but our own learning allows us to adapt what we do so that we can best support others. With that in mind, within the following chapters we will explore; how to sequence and scaffold learning, how to plan purposeful, focussed lessons and how to model positive attitudes and behaviours. We will also consider theories such as metacognition and cognitive load in relation to how we support learners to achieve their very best. This is not a complete menu of course, it is simply an appetiser, there is much more to discover within.

We have called this book the *Ultimate Lesson Planner*, and we hope that the title illustrates the content. It is a book that comes from experience, and between us we have over 100 years' worth of teaching in a variety of subject areas! It isn't easy to encapsulate that amount of expertise in a single text, so we have tried to focus on the key elements of teaching a lesson and to do this we designed the chapters around a typical lesson plan. Whilst we appreciate that formats for plans vary, most of them will include the following elements:

- Learning aims and objectives;
- Starting the lesson;

- Resources and activities;
- Adapting learning;
- Checking learning;
- Challenging thinking;
- Embedding additional skills;
- Concluding the lesson.

All of these things are important considerations in planning, and each element will enable you to prepare a lesson which is both purposeful and enjoyable. That said, we also recognise that a lesson plan (however well prepared it is) is not a universal guarantee that the lesson will go as intended. That's fine, nothing in life is perfect and our approach is to embrace those 'imperfections' and see every mishap as an opportunity. For this reason, we have included a section in each of the chapters entitled 'learn from our experience'. Here we explore real events, which mostly didn't go 'according to plan' and consider the reasons for this, as well as what we might have done differently.

When we were planning this project, an important determinant for the content was the ways in which teaching has changed over the years, especially in terms of the growing use and importance of information technology in the classroom. For the most part, teachers now work with digital natives, the inhabitants of generation Z who were born between 2001 and 2020. These are the people who have grown up with computers and access to the internet, for whom the use of technology is an integral part of daily life. Unlike earlier generations, this group views the world first through a technological lens, so it makes sense to use this to our advantage. In spite of the inception of the Internet, search engines that allow students to find information at the touch of a key and the development of robots with artificial intelligence (who may be able to write essays or even mark exams in the future), we don't believe that technology will be replacing teachers any time soon, and don't always think that digital learning is the best approach, but we absolutely do acknowledge its value in supporting teaching and learning. In recognition of this, we have included a dedicated section in each chapter entitled 'leveraging learning technology'. Here we will explain how you might use technology to best effect in a particular part of the lesson, and we have supported this with some additional resources you can access straight away.

Finally, we recognise that learning doesn't only take place in the classroom, it goes far beyond that space, we learn in a variety of situations, and we need to capitalise on that opportunity. Individualising learning through the use of specific and challenging goals is an important strategy which can have a significant impact on motivation and performance and for this reason, our final chapter explores this very topic.

We planned this book with you in mind. If you are, or have been, the teacher caught out by a passing comment in the staff room, the teacher who was so dedicated, they took on something that scared them, the teacher who is prepared to get it wrong, knowing that this will help you to get it right. Or maybe you are the teacher who knows that 'right' and 'wrong' are just opinions and that the important thing is to do something well, to be as skilful and considered as you can, whatever the circumstances. If you are that teacher, then this book is for you.

1 Why plan?

Introduction

'If you fail to prepare you are preparing to fail' is a well-known saying which extols the virtues of thinking ahead. Like any good aphorism, the simplicity of its message contains a general truth, and it would be difficult to find an argument against it. Yet, when we see others in action it is not unusual to be taken in by the ease with which they carry out their roles, so much so, we may be persuaded to think their performance is fuelled by natural flair rather than preparation, particularly when it comes to classroom practice. 'Teachers are born not made' right? These teachers often make their practice look effortless; a natural skill that they just happen to be blessed with – but don't be fooled by that. In our experience, great teachers, teachers who have an impact, understand their subject and how it is learnt, present content in ways which activate learners' thinking and create supportive learning environments (Coe et al., 2020). This rarely happens by accident. Great teachers spend a lot of time thinking about their teaching and readily acknowledge the importance of good planning.

Without a doubt, teachers can have a transformational impact on their students' lives. Teachers not only impart knowledge, they influence learners' beliefs about what they are able to achieve and this goes far beyond the classroom. Research suggests that the long-term impact is represented in overall level of education, salary, and lifetime income (Chetty et al., 2014) You probably guessed that already ... but it is good to have it confirmed. Whilst we cannot dismiss the impact of socio-economic factors on learner achievement, there is further evidence to suggest that this gap can be reduced by good teaching (Slater et al., 2012) so in a nutshell ... teachers matter!

Why plan?

If teaching is to have an impact, then it must also have a clear purpose, especially if 'impact' is measured via practical achievements. For most teachers (at least those who work in formal teaching environments), the purpose of lessons will be closely linked to learners' expected outcomes, for example, preparation for assessment or the development of specific skills. In addition, teaching is about preparation for life, so it also includes the development of soft skills such as communication, managing time, working with others and developing

DOI: 10.4324/9781003385905-2

independence. Detailed planning certainly provides the opportunity to focus learning and to think about how you include the additional elements of a lesson, but it also creates the space for some flexibility. It is important to remember that a plan is just that … a plan … it is not a set of rules that must be adhered to or a tick list of activities to complete. Great lesson plans have built-in flexibility so that you can exploit those 'teachable moments' as and when they present themselves.

There are different approaches to lesson planning and even some trends related to how teaching should be structured. These ideas will be discussed in more detail in later chapters, but for now, let's assume that approaches to planning will be based on what we believe about learning. So your initial questions might be:

- What do I want students to learn?
- How can they best learn that?
- How will I know what they have learnt?

You might also be thinking about other aspects of learning which are not directly assessed, such as how learners interact with one another or how motivated they are and how you can build in opportunities for these things. None of this will happen by magic, it all needs to be considered at the planning stage.

Figure 1.1 Beware of lurking dragons

An important point to note in all aspects of planning is that plans very often don't play out exactly as expected, and as experienced teachers we have all been in situations when we've had to think on our feet and alter the plan to make sure that it achieves the intended aims. Unless you are teaching one learner at a time, it is likely that every class will have a mix of abilities, attitudes and motivations which influence the way they learn. For this reason, it is essential you get to know your learners and plan for any potential hurdles which may be presented, as Tolkien says: 'It does not do to leave a live dragon out of your calculations, if you live near one' (Tolkien, 2013:268).

Detailed planning not only helps things to run smoothly, it also helps you to prepare for lurking dragons (Figure 1.1)!

The social and emotional aspects of learning

An important part of planning is thinking about how you create a safe and stimulating class-room environment. It is very easy to focus all of your attention on the content of a lesson, the 'how' and 'what' elements. That makes absolute sense – we all want to teach the right things in the most effective way, but we also want to ensure that we create in our learners a desire for knowledge and an interest in learning itself: 'The most valuable thing a teacher can impart is not the knowledge and understanding per se but a *longing* for knowledge and understanding' (Einstein in Calaprice, 2011:101). Motivation is important, so too is the feeling of security learners find in a positive classroom environment and that means giving thought to the different dimensions of learning. According to Illeris (2009), there are three key elements:

- Content – what and how is taught. This is often framed in statements about knowledge and skills but may include attitudes such as showing respect for peers.
- Incentive – has a focus on drive towards learning so it includes our feelings, and motivation.
- Interaction – often described as the 'social' element, encompassing interactions with teachers and peers.

By recognising all of these elements we are more likely to teach the right things in the best way taking into account how individual learners might experience the learning.

The importance of sequencing teaching

When I [Lydia] was at school, which I must admit was a very long time ago, my history teacher taught me a mnemonic (BROM), which he insisted would help me to remember the order of battles in a particular war, stating that it was an essential piece of knowledge if I was going to pass my A level exam. I passed the exam and to this day I remember the sequence and the names of the battles (Blenheim, Ramillies, Oudenarde and Malplaquet), but – although I knew it at the time – I have no idea at all today which war was being fought, who was fighting or why. The fact is simply an isolated island of remembered knowledge floating around in my long-term memory because I was simply taught to remember some-thing without any real understanding or context.

I also studied English to A level, which brought me into contact with Shakespeare's plays. At the start of the course, I hated it. I put all the barriers up, I found the language difficult, the plots non-sensical (I had to study the rather far-fetched plot of the *Tempest*, which didn't help) and I couldn't see why anyone would choose to write in poetry rather than prose. I was, however, blessed with an exceptional teacher who not only loved his subject but who had, by the end of the course, instilled into his students (including me!) if not a love of Shakespeare, at least an understanding and appreciation of his works.

Why the difference? Both were good teachers, but they began their teaching from different starting points. Starting the history course was a bit like being parachuted into the unknown; he concentrated solely on the subject matter, dealing with facts, dates and sequences of events of nineteenth-century European history. My English teacher started by talking about Shakespeare, who he was and when he lived. He started with a play with a plot line that wasn't too difficult to follow (*Julius Caesar*) making connections with historical facts and explaining how plays were produced at the time, what theatres looked like and so on, making connections between historical reality and the fiction of the play itself. In doing this he gave us a foundation on which to build our knowledge of the play which enabled him to gradually lead us through the really difficult bit – understanding the Shakespearean language – and showing us its relevance by explaining how some of the words and expressions we use now are derived from the plays themselves.

My history teacher was teaching using a somewhat directive method of teaching – expecting us all to be able to repeat elements of 'knowledge' acquired through rote learning. My English teacher adopted a different method – that of allowing us all to learn as individuals by developing schemas. I don't know if he knew he was following the classical learning theory developed by Piaget and Cook (1952), but by giving us a basic underpinning knowledge (the schema) of the subject he enabled us to connect new elements to firm foundations. Each time a new fact, word or idea was introduced in the lesson we were able to attach it to something we already knew, so our schema developed – a bit like throwing a pebble in a pond, the waves this creates spread out, but they are all connected to the splash caused by the pebble going into the water.

The basic concept of a schema is really very simple – it's a frame or structure to which we can attach something else but an understanding of how these can be built can be a very useful tool in the teacher's armoury at various levels. Initially, when starting to plan for a group of lessons the teacher needs to decide on the starting point. Lots of factors need to be taken into consideration when identifying this, for example, the type of students, their current level of understanding of the subject matter (if any) and their readiness to learn (Knowles et al., 1998). Once you have a handle of these factors your planning for great lessons can really take off.

Obviously, the subject matter is going to be a primary factor in your planning as is the organisation of the subject matter, so that new information is linked to previous learning which is already familiar. Why is it important that learners develop their individual schema? Well, as Gardner (1991) argues we have different minds and because of this, construct our learning in different ways. For example, one of our learners is a very divergent thinker and uses her imagination to relate learning to the growth of a tree – each piece of new information is a leaf, which she initially connects to a twig attached to the main trunk. As her knowledge grows so the twigs become branches with new twigs growing from them to which further leaves are added. Another works differently, creating his schema more logically using lists or arrows which point from one piece of information to another, yet another prefers to use mind maps using colours to connect thoughts and ideas. All of these are equally effective but the way they develop the schema is very personal to the student.

Scaffolding

Once the sequence of teaching and learning has been established teachers can use their knowledge and skills to help their learners develop their individual schemas by scaffolding the learning process. Initially learners need a firm base to work from. The role of the teacher here is one of leadership - the teacher must plan to lead learning by presenting basic facts, concepts or other information in manageable, connected 'chunks' to form the foundation of a schema. Once established the role of the teacher, and consequently the way in which they plan their lessons, can move from a transmission model of teaching to an approach in which learners are more actively engaged in the learning process. As the teacher leads their learners across what Vygotsky (1978) describes as the Zone of Proximal Development (ZPD) (moving from the known to the unknown) - the teacher 'scaffolds' (Bruner, 1960) the learning process by adding support and guidance where it is needed. Although still planning and leading the learning process, the teacher has moved to a more supportive role, that of a *More Knowledgeable Other* (Vygotsky, 1978) helping learners to develop their schema by gradually encouraging them to take an increasing amount of responsibility for their learning. This is done by incorporating things such as interactive activities, group work, independent research or games into their planning to encourage learners to assimilate new information into their existing schema in their own way. Initially the teacher will have to plan to guide and monitor these activities closely but as learners' confidence increases the level of support or scaffolding can be reduced.

As learners develop their schemas individually this can be quite a challenge for the teacher. It is relatively easy to plan for group activities, but it is not so easy to plan to help an individual who may be struggling to add something new into their existing schema. This situation requires a degree of spontaneity on the part of the teacher who may need to move quickly back to transmission teaching or, sometimes more effectively, to implement 'Plan B'. Almost all teachers will have developed a Plan B for the lesson whilst they were preparing their definitive lesson plan. Although they will have thought about and planned the use of different strategies to explain the subject matter, maybe through using a mind map, a video, a game or even, as we have done in this chapter, a story used to illustrate key learning, this is Plan A. Plan B is the list of activities which have not 'made the cut' when selecting resources for the lesson but remain in reserve in case they are needed. These may not appear on the lesson plan itself - they may simply remain in the teacher's head, but they are a form of planning and most good teachers recognise that however detailed your initial planning, there are times when it simply won't work as planned - this is when Plan B may well save the day!

Plan B

All of this might seem a little overwhelming. Not only are we suggesting that you need a detailed lesson plan which covers key subject content, keeps your learners actively engaged and develops a few soft skills; we are now saying you also need a back-up plan! True – but we want to assure you that this need not be too time-consuming. Over time, you will build up a wealth of resources you can tap into, so much so you could probably have a plan C or D should it be required. In the meantime, we are going to share with you some generic strategies which you may be able to adapt for your own subject and you can find these though this link.

The need for flexibility

Routine is an important part of anyone's day and for most of us, our daily routines are something we rarely question, so much so, we often can't remember the reasons why we do things in the way that we do. This of course carries through to our work, where we tend to structure the working day in similar ways and very probably develop our own 'formula' for teaching a class. This can be a very good thing, especially when it comes to managing your time; however, it can also be constraining as we rely on what we 'know' works with the consequent danger that learners become bored and are less likely to engage when experiencing the same routine every time they see you.

Learn from our experience

This reflection is part of a conversation overheard during a coffee break in in staffroom:

They all trooped in for the lesson, sat down in the same places, waiting for the handout. But one was missing – the 'bright spark' who always had something to say. No one seemed to know where he was so I just carried on and taught the lesson as normal, asking them what they remembered from last time and then going through the PowerPoint, explaining everything in detail so they could take notes before they all left for the next lesson. They're not a very attentive lot and not many of them seemed to be taking notes. I later found the missing student loitering in the corridor and asked why he hadn't been in the lesson – cheeky little so-and-so said he didn't need to come – all he had to do was pick up the PowerPoints and look at the notes section. Why do I bother?

Well, it appears from the anecdote above that the teacher had prepared and taught the lesson, so why was the 'bright spark' bored? Possibly because he knew what to expect in terms of how the lesson would be taught. The teacher had prepared a detailed PowerPoint and gone through it point by point. We can see how that might appear to be a very thorough approach and something which made the teacher feel confident they had covered every-thing that needed to be covered, but would it have been more interesting for the learners if, instead of 'teacher talk' some activities had been included? Or perhaps a demonstration? There are lots of approaches to take, but it is very easy to get comfortable with a particular way of doing things, forgetting that this might not be the best approach for others.

According to Mezirow (1991), there can be significant value in shaking up our routines and challenging our thinking in order to open up new ways of looking at things. Honest reflec-tion on our practice is one way of doing this as it provides an opportunity to take a step back from the habitual and explore some options. This teacher was using methods he was comfortable with and which focussed almost entirely on the content of the lesson. If he had thought about all the things Illeris pointed out earlier in the chapter, the need to take note of feelings and motivation and the interaction between learners and teachers (something very obviously lacking in the story above) he could have incentivised the learning by altering his plan to actively include the learners.

The value of mishaps

Teaching can sometimes feel like an exposed profession. It is a job that is subject to much judgement from others, perhaps rightly so. It is an important undertaking – teachers play such a significant part in shaping the minds of young people, and in turn liberating (or constraining) thought. In doing so, teachers have the power to enhance or limit freedom. It is no wonder that we sometimes feel a little vulnerable. In addition, just about *everyone* you meet seems to know how best to teach, or at least it seems that way. Given these factors it is understandable that some new teachers are very conscious of their practice and some-what reluctant to highlight anything they consider to be less than perfect. Although this is a perfectly natural reaction, it is something we feel may limit development and we would encourage you to acknowledge and value your mistakes. Mishaps happen – everyone has 'bad' lessons, most teachers could attest to any number of mistakes in both the planning and execution of lessons, and we are happy to share some of ours with you:

- Losing control of the class;
- Running significantly over time;
- Inadvertently excluding some learners;

- Bending down without realising that your clothing revealed more than it should;
- Forgetting to turn your phone off and being unable to find it;
- Spilling coffee on a student's beautifully presented work;
- Rushing around the room and tripping over something.

If we thought about this long enough, we could probably fill a few pages. The key message here is, no one is perfect, and no one is expected to be. What is most important about mishaps is our ability to learn from these events. For this reason, as we have done in the 'learn from our experience' section, we will be sharing some of our stories throughout the following chapters.

Peer observation

For this activity you will be carrying out an observation of one of your peers. Peer observation can be a very beneficial tool in encouraging reflection, challenging thinking and widening perspectives. Seeing others' teaching can support personal reflection as well as help generate new ideas for your practice, so think carefully about who you might like to observe. Perhaps someone who teaches a different subject or takes an alternative approach? To get the most out of the activity it is important that the focus is on your own learning, therefore you need to adopt a non-judgemental stance and we would recommend using the 'stolen goods' method to structure and record your observation. To do this, you simply answer three questions:

- Things I have noticed;
- Things I would like to steal from you;
- Things I would like to offer you.

Observations are also more productive if they have a focus so perhaps select an aspect of a lesson you would like to concentrate on, for example, chunking material or scaffolding. When you have carried out your observation, why not ask your colleague if they would be willing to observe you?

Whilst we have advocated the importance of taking a flexible approach, we also recognise that some of our routines are a force for good as they provide a framework from which to work. Challenging thinking is simply about exploring our assumptions and it is very likely that after carrying out a peer observation you will reflect on things you want to change. It is equally likely that you will recognise many positive aspects of your teaching that you can continue to build on.

Summary

In this chapter we have discussed the importance of planning for teaching and more importantly for learning. To do this effectively it is important to understand how we learn and, as teachers, how we can organise lessons in ways which support this process for every learner. When you take into account the individual level at which we learn, this can seem quite a daunting task and you may well be wondering how you will be able to build in support mechanisms for every single learner within every single class. It isn't easy … but, there are a number of strategies you can employ and these will be explored in the following chapters.

References

Brookfield, S. (1995) *Becoming a Critically Reflective Practitioner.* San Francisco: Jossey-Bass.

Bruner, J. S. (1960) *The Process of Education.* Cambridge, MA: Harvard Press

Calaprice, A. (2011) *The Ultimate Quotable Einstein.* Princeton, NJ: Princeton University Press.

Chetty, R., Friedman, J. N. and Rockoff, J. E. (2014) 'Measuring the Impact of Teachers II: Teacher Value-Added and Student Outcomes in Adulthood', *American Economic Review,* 104(9): 2633–2679. http://dx.doi.org/10.1257/aer.104.9.2633.

Coe, P., Rauch, C. J., Kime, S. and Singleton, D. (2020) Great Teaching Toolkit. Available online 5ee9f507021911ae35ac6c4d_EBE_GTT_EVIDENCE REVIEW_DIGITAL.pdf (website-files.com)

Gardner, H. (1991) *The Unschooled Mind: How Children Think and How Schools Should Teach.* New York: Basic Books.

Illeris, K. (2009) *Contemporary Theories of Learning, Learning Theorists … In Their Own Words.* Oxford: Routledge.

Knowles, M. S., Elwood, R. Holton III, R. and Swanson, A. (1998) *The Adult Learner: The Definitive Classic in Adult Education and Human Resource Development.* 5th edition, New York: Heinemann.

Mezirow, J. (1991) *Transformative Dimensions of Adult Learning.* San Francisco, CA: Jossey-Bass.

Piaget, J. and Cook, M. T. (1952) *The Origins of Intelligence in Children.* New York, NY: International University Press.

Slater, H., Davies, N. M. and Burgess, S. (2012) 'Do Teachers Matter? Measuring the Variation in Teacher Effectiveness in England', *Oxford Bulletin of Economics and Statistics,* 74(5): 0305–9049. doi: 10.1111/j.1468-0084.2011.00666.x

Tolkien, J. R. R. (2013) *The Hobbit or There and Back Again* (illustrated edition). London: Harper Collins.

Vygotsky, L. S. (1978) *Mind in Society: The Development of Higher Psychological Processes.* Cambridge, MA: Harvard University Press.

2 Learning aims and objectives

Introduction

Imagine you are going on a journey ... let's assume it's a long-awaited adventure with specific things you want to see and do. You have high hopes for the experience, maybe even expect it to change your life! With such a journey, it is very likely you would check out the best route, consider travel time and pack everything you think you might need along the way. Your plans might include a general direction of travel, some very specific aims and the necessary resources to get you from A to B, not dissimilar to how you might embark on planning a lesson!

Planning lessons is an essential part of the teaching role – indeed it is the main focus of this book and in this chapter we are going to consider the way in which a lesson plan provides a 'route map' for teaching. In doing so, the plan makes connections to the general landscape of the subject or topic, as well as outlining specific pointers along the way.

Sequencing lesson content

It can be difficult to know where to start with lesson planning and the skill is something that will evolve over time. In truth, it is quite a personal thing and the specific format chosen to map out the plan will vary depending on your preferences. Some people like to have lots of detail and others prefer a more skeletal approach, but before you make your mind up about that, it might be wise to have some initial structure. A familiar strategy for structuring lessons is the ABC three-part plan – this consists of:

A – The start
B – The main body
C – The plenary

Although this seems quite obvious, having ABC in mind does provide a framework for the main parts of the lesson and ensures you think about how the lesson is introduced and concluded as well as the specific content you want to cover. You would be surprised how many people simply focus on the main content and forget to 'top and tail' the lesson. Whilst the ABC model won't guarantee a perfect lesson, it will provide a positive start and will help

DOI: 10.4324/9781003385905-3

you to plan something with enough detail to guide the process, as well as the flexibility you may need if you have to switch to plan B during the lesson.

Communicating clear belief in learners' potential

As with any journey, it is important that we make a positive start and that means getting our learners in the right frame of mind. They must be motivated and ready to learn. They also need to feel that their efforts will be rewarded ... that what they do will result in learning. In other words, they need to receive the message that they are *able to* learn.

Cultivating an environment where high expectations are the norm helps learners to see that the teacher believes in their ability, which in turn supports belief in themselves. The term often used to describe this is 'self-fulfilling prophecy'. This refers to a process whereby individual beliefs and subsequent expectations lead to behaviours which reinforce the original belief. This is best illustrated by the well-known aphorism, 'whether you believe you can do a thing or not, you are right' (a quote typically accredited to Henry Ford but apparently appearing first as a filler item in the *Reader's Digest* in 1947). This idea was transported to an education setting through the original work of Rosenthal and Jacobson (1968) and is an idea that researchers and educators have continued to build on. Rosenthal and Jacobson recognised that teacher expectations had a significant influence on student performance and (perhaps inadvertently) gave weight to the self-fulfilling prophecies individual learners had developed in relation to their ability. Put simply, when teachers expressed positive expectations, this influenced performance in a positive way and negative expectations did the opposite. This popular theory became known as the 'Pygmalion effect': 'When we expect certain behaviours of others, we are likely to act in ways that make the expected behaviour more likely to occur' (Rosenthal and Babad, 1985:36).

Understandably, this idea has much appeal, especially when we think we might be able to influence achievement simply by having, and expressing, more faith in our learners. At a superficial level that seems like a small act of magic! But how much influence does teacher expectation really have on learners' performance? Although there have been some criticisms of the original work in this field, and subsequent debate about the extent of the impact of teacher expectations, there is evidence to suggest that 'self-fulfilling prophecies' in the classroom are real and that the messages teachers convey about their expectations do matter (Jussim and Harber, 2005). That said, this is in no way a quick fix, we don't simply tell our learners we have high expectations of them, we have to show this through consistent behaviours which demonstrate our faith in them. Not only does what we do and say at the start of a lesson influence our learners' motivation, it will positively influence their belief in their ability to learn successfully, so it makes sense to set high expectations from the outset.

Modelling values, attitudes and behaviours

Setting high expectations isn't just about the outcomes of learning – it is also about the process, so at the beginning of each and every class it is important that teachers model the values, attitudes and behaviours they want to see in their classroom. This provides an example of expectations and creates a sense of security for learners within the class. By modelling values such as respect and inclusivity, we are giving the message that the classroom is a safe place and that is essential if we want the environment to be a positive one. Pro-social modelling describes the specific behaviours of positive role models such as, developing good relationships, modelling desired behaviours, using effective reinforcement and communicating attitudes in thinking. This means that if teachers want their learners to be punctual, prepared for learning, respectful of others and collaborative then they need to demonstrate all of those things in their own actions. It seems a very simple task, but we suspect that most people are not paragons and at some point we all slip up. The key thing is awareness … if we know that what we are doing isn't working, then we need to understand why before we can change it.

Imagine you have just started working with a new group of learners and your close colleague has given you a very detailed account of the group's lack of respect and general belligerence. How is this likely to influence how you behave with them? What initial expectations are you likely to have? How would you prepare yourself?

Be honest in your initial reflection.

Then try to flip the scenario around – what if you assumed your colleague was wrong? What if you decided that this was a highly motivated group ready to learn? How might you prepare your lesson? What expectations will you convey?

By reframing the information we have about students, we are likely to behave differently towards them and often find they respond differently to us. Your colleague may well be absolutely right about the group … but this strategy is well worth a try. As suggested by the Pygmalion effect, how we treat others and the expectations we convey all have an impact.

The importance of classroom environment can't be stated strongly enough and there is much literature to support this, some of which has been summarised in Table 2.1 where we have provided an 'in a nutshell' overview with examples of theory in practice.

If those studies don't convince you, there is even more to justify the importance of taking time to get the environment right. Further evidence suggests that supportive classrooms are also associated with positive learner outcomes. Dweck's well-known work on 'Growth Mindset' (2017) suggests that instilling a sense of 'self-belief' and 'untapped potential' has a positive impact on achievement especially in relation to effort. Similarly, teacher expectations, communicated through unconscious behaviour can also have a significant impact. But it is worth remembering that the 'subtle unconscious' messages we give out may not always be positive. Teachers, unknowingly interact differently with different students through a range of behaviours, for example, more smiling, nodding and eye contact with students we expect to do well, whilst offering more emotional support to those students for whom we may have low expectations (Murdock-Perriera and Sedlacek, 2018)

Table 2.1 Theory to practice

The theory	In a nutshell	In practice
Ryan and Deci 2000 *Self-determination theory*	Focussed on the 'why' of behaviour and considers basic psychological needs such as autonomy, feelings of competence, relatedness. When the environment is supportive of these needs, motivation is considered to be intrinsic and acts as a positive driver.	Psychological needs may be supported by: • Autonomy – providing choice in the classroom. • Competence – providing challenging (but not overwhelming goals) and recognising achievement. • Relatedness – creating a sense of mutual support.
Nakamura and Csikzentmihalyi 2003 *Meaningful engagement*	Focussed on providing learners with a sense of autonomy. Another important factor is that learning should be seen as relevant in order to increase overall engagement.	• Supporting independent learning by providing adapted tasks (with more or less guidance depending on need). • Ensuring classroom activities are meaningful and connected to overall learning. • Emphasising links to employability and real world experiences.
Bandura 1996 *Self-efficacy theory*	Focussed on one's own self-belief and ability to achieve goals. In turn, this leads to increased commitment and perseverance in working towards goals.	• Providing the opportunity for mastery of learning using activities which build upon on another and reinforce key learning. • Creating an environment which acknowledges success and allows vicarious experience. By seeing peers succeed, it is easier to believe in own abilities. • Verbal persuasion – by using clear communication to provide feedback and guidance, learners can be supported through tasks and will be motivated to make an effort. • Acknowledging emotional state – a positive mood can boost self-efficacy, but anxiety can undermine it. Reducing stressful situations and capitalising on positive events can help create a positive environment.

The teacher's impact on motivation

Setting out expectations at the beginning of a lesson has a number of benefits. It lets learners know what is expected of them, demonstrates how the lesson is likely to proceed and provides a taster of what they will be learning. Not only is this an organised approach to starting your class, it also provides motivation for your learners, especially if they can see how the new learning fits in with their overall aims.

Motivation as a word is in regular, perhaps habitual, use. On the surface, we all know what it means to be motivated or otherwise, but like many cognitive processes, it can be difficult to recognise in others and even more difficult to inspire. Motivation is a derivative of the Latin 'to move' and in a teaching and learning context this is exactly how we want to use it ... we want to move our learners to activity, to get involved in lessons, to apply themselves and ultimately to achieve their goals. This should be straightforward enough, but we also need to remember that motivation can be both intrinsic (from internal sources) and extrinsic (from external sources) and of course we don't have control over all of the things our students experience. Therefore, the aim for most teachers is to consider how they might leverage the motivation process in order to enhance learning outcomes. Most theories related to motivation are focussed on the direction of behaviour within a given context. In teaching, which is a socially driven environment, this usually means there is a social and cognitive foundation influencing how and why learners are motivated. Important considerations are:

- The individual's self-perception (Am I a 'good' learner?);
- Perceived value/interest in an activity (Is this in the assignment? Is this interesting?);
- How success and failure is attributed (Who/what is the reason for my success/failure?);
- A focus on achievement desires/needs (Do I want/need to achieve this?).

What is important to remember is that all of these things can be influenced by teachers in ways which positively affect learner outcomes and there are a number of simple strategies that can be employed from the outset (Lazowski and Hulleman, 2016).

The ARCS model (Keller, 1987) outlines four simple components of student motivation, these are:

- Attention;
- Relevance;
- Confidence;
- Satisfaction.

Attention – Getting, and maintaining learners' attention at the beginning of a lesson is essential, which is why the start is key in setting the overall tone. In Chapter 3 we outline a number of strategies you can use for a positive start but remember an exciting start only goes so far. You need to maintain a level of interest throughout the lesson so using a variety of teaching strategies and resources is important.

Relevance – Whatever the age group you are working with, learners want to know the relevance of what they are learning, they need to know why the learning is important and how it relates to the 'bigger picture'. Although, for most teachers learning is valuable in and of itself, learners are very often focussed on overall outcomes, so why not make those connections at the outset? This is also an important consideration when designing activities ... they should be engaging and fun to complete but if they are not relevant, they simply become fillers and will probably have a negative effect on overall motivation.

Confidence – Learner confidence is often related to beliefs about the possibility of success, so opportunities for success should be built into your lesson. Adapting activities for different needs, or putting in discrete support means you are setting your learners up for success, rather than failure.

Satisfaction – Learners want to be satisfied with what they have achieved during the process, so we need to build in opportunities to recognise achievements. This could take the form of a reflection on learning, or perhaps peer feedback. Sometimes a simple 'well done' is effective, that small recognition can make a big difference.

Aims and objectives

A practical strategy for setting out lesson expectations is through the use of aims and objectives. These are the general and specific statements used to convey the intent of learning. So an aim might be used to communicate an end goal, such as 'demonstrate an understanding of the skeletal system', whereas an objective would be a specific statement about what a learner might be able to do whilst working towards the aim, for example, 'name the 27 bones in the hand'. We provide some more specific examples in the section on writing objectives. Some of us may recall that these simple statements were once viewed as the 'holy grail' of a well-planned lesson. Indeed, without clearly written learning objectives a lesson could hardly be considered worthwhile! The message inculcated in teacher training was that specific and measurable learning objectives were essential to good teaching. In addition, these statements had to be shared with learners and the beginning of the lesson and reviewed and the end ... and for good measure, perhaps visited and 'ticked-off' somewhere in the middle. So strong was this message that teachers and learners were complicit in their adherence to it and both seemed somewhat put out if they were not present ... but why?

Learn from our experience

This excerpt is taken from an experience of one of the authors, so is written as a personal reflection.

In the spirit of encouraging autonomy and reducing reliance on teacher guidance, I decided to structure my lesson in a different way. The rationale behind this was that the change to 'business as usual' might prompt my group to start thinking about the reasons why we do things in certain ways and in turn consider alternative approaches. Based on this premise, I created a lesson focussed on reflection where individuals could share their professional concerns and through the group process try to establish some creative solutions. The first step was to set the scene, so I told the group that there would be no learning objectives for the lesson. This was met with concerned glances from one to the other, the tapping of pens on the desk and other indicators of discomfort. I noticed that one student wrote 'NO OBJECTIVES' on the top of his notepad, followed by a series of 'bullet points' where presumably he would have written the expected statements.

This is a true story based in the context of teacher education, where we might assume that the learners, as trainee teachers, would be open to, if not expecting, a range of approaches to teaching. The initial tension in the room was palpable, suggesting that even for high-achieving individuals, there is comfort in routine. We have all been using objectives for so long we have forgotten why – they have just become a part of the unwritten contract of how a lesson should be. Perhaps this is because of how we were taught or maybe because in previous inspection regimes, such statements were considered to have a close connection to learning. Whatever the reason, it is worth dispelling the myth that stating and revisiting learning objectives is a factor in how much or how well people learn, and with that in mind we should consider their real purpose so that we might use them to best effect.

In most cases, learning programmes will have specified outcomes which show what participants will have learnt or be able to do by the end of the course. This is further broken down into specific units, to represent different topics, or chunks of learning and then into individual lessons. This is helpful not only in providing an overall map for the learning journey but in highlighting landmarks we need to visit along the way and without this breakdown, we might be venturing into unknown territory. This is illustrated in *Alice's Adventures in Wonderland*.

> 'Would you tell me, please, which way I ought to go from here?'
> 'That depends a good deal on where you want to get to,' said the Cat.
> 'I don't much care where' – said Alice.
> 'Then it doesn't matter which way you go,' said the Cat.

The conversation between Alice and the Cheshire Cat in *Alice's Adventures in Wonderland* (Carroll, 2021) is an example of this. Alice has no idea where she should go. The cat, doesn't know either, leaving her wondering what she should do, and like the example presented earlier in the chapter, this could cause a certain amount of discomfort. When we are exploring the territory in Wonderland, or exploring our own reflections, that may not be a bad thing – but when we are working towards a specific aim and need to arrive at a particular destination, then it is reassuring to know that our direction of travel is correct.

For most teachers, the key focus is on ensuring that their learners develop knowledge and skills as they learn and to do this teachers need to think about two things; 'What do my learners need to know/be able to do?' and 'How do I know they know/can do this?' By outlining specific objectives for each lesson, a teacher is able to specify the direction of learning as well as measure whether or not learning has taken place.

Writing learning objectives

If the key purpose of learning objectives is to specify learning intent and provide a way of measuring whether learning has taken place, then the language used must be precise. This seems like a simple enough thing but it is often surprising how difficult it can be to define exactly what learning will look like. A common approach used is to state what learners will be able to do at the end of a lesson, for example: 'At the end of the lesson learners should be able to name the 27 bones in the hand.' So far, so good, but what if they need knowledge of how the bones and muscles interact, or perhaps they are expected to consider the differences between the hands and the feet? This would require higher levels of thinking that might be more difficult to define. One way of doing this easily is to use action verbs which pinpoint specifically what we are looking for, for example at a lower level we might want learners to name, list or identify, but if a deeper understanding is required it is probable we will want them to interpret, deduce or analyse.

Taxonomies of learning

Although developed more than 50 years ago, Bloom's Taxonomy (1965) is still a useful tool in helping us to devise meaningful objectives. This taxonomy is based on the idea that there are levels within the cognitive 'domain' (the part of our brain that develops mental skills and knowledge), and that specific verbs can be used to define different levels of thinking. In Figure 2.1 we have adapted Blooms' model to describe the skills which may be demonstrated at the various stages of the taxonomy. At the simplest level this shows skills such as being able to recall information, to more complex actions such as analysis and creation, depicting each of them as individual levels.

The model itself has had a number of iterations, and there is some debate about the order of the levels presented. In the version we are using here, evaluation is seen as one of the highest-level skills, yet we can evaluate by simply making a choice between some options, in which case it isn't a particularly complex skill. Whilst this type of taxonomy is a useful tool in terms of defining learning, it should be stressed that learning does not necessarily happen in a linear way and of course when we produce a model in the form of a hierarchy, there is the suggestion that the things at the bottom are less important. This is certainly not the case. In most subjects there are key things, in the form of threshold knowledge that we need to learn. In this model, they would fit into the knowledge category (shown here as the first step of the model) but that doesn't mean they are the lowest level skill; they are actually fundamental to the subject itself. It isn't a perfect model but when used in the right way, it can be very helpful.

The taxonomy we have included here is based on the cognitive domain, and as you can see from the verbs used in the example, it refers to a range of thinking processes. Learning doesn't end there, of course, and many of you will also need to write objectives

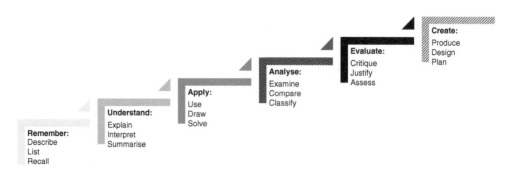

Figure 2.1 Bloom's taxonomy

relating to different types of learning such as practical skills (which are part of the psycho-motor domain) or interpersonal skills (in the affective domain). The importance of these may vary depending on your teaching context, but one domain that is fundamental to generating a positive approach to learning is the affective domain. This domain includes the ways in which we deal with emotions, therefore it influences how we manage ourselves, how we interact with others, our motivations, attitudes and evolving values. These things are embedded in the learning process and in our view should be included in planning in much the same way as we would plan for knowledge-based objectives. We would even go as far as to say that every successful learning event involves both cognitive and affective processes.

Earlier in the chapter we talked about how Alice got lost in the woods and the discomfort this would have caused her because she didn't have any idea which route to take. In order to deal with this feeling in a positive way, she would need to recognise the importance of 'being lost' and acknowledge that this might be the first step to getting to where she needed to be. Alice also had to be adaptable and resilient as she experienced a number of things outside of her usual comfort zone; somewhat familiar but not quite as they seemed. When she plays croquet with the Queen of Hearts she is experiencing something she might ordinarily do in her above ground life, but she:

> had never seen such a curious croquet-ground in her life: it was all ridges and furrows: the croquet balls were live hedgehogs and the mallets live flamingoes, and the soldiers had to double themselves up and stand on their hands and feet, to make the arches.
>
> (Carroll, 2021:66)

Perhaps not a pleasant experience for a girl used to a more genteel approach to the game. To participate at all, she had to develop a belief in herself and learn to embrace the unexpected. Perhaps the most important thing Alice learnt was to be curious, about her surroundings, about others and about herself. In essence, Alice's adventure had provided her with the opportunity to develop a range of skills which required her to receive and respond to unexpected experiences (Figure 2.2).

Affective domain

The affective domain contains five stages:

Receiving – Being aware of phenomena, feelings and emotions. This is the first step to any new learning in this domain.

Responding – Actively participating in the process and reacting to stimuli. This might be having a conversation, complying with requests and so on.

Valuing – Attaching worth to a particular object, phenomenon or behaviour. Accepting a level of commitment to something

Organising – Putting together values, information and ideas to bring about a consistent philosophy/belief structure.

Characterising – Internalising values and acting consistently in accordance with them.

How might these skills be demonstrated in your subject? What could you do in your lesson to help your learners to develop skills in this domain?

Figure 2.2 What Alice learnt

Sharing information about the lesson

As you can see from the 'learn from our experience' story, there are certain expectations around learning objectives and at some point you need to decide how these will be used within your own lessons. Sharing the intended learning seems like a good idea, it presents an overview of the lesson, shows some specific things to be learnt and may motivate your learners. On the other hand, a long list of objectives may present itself as a mountain to climb. One thing to remember is that learning objectives are generally set by the teacher which means they tend to be focussed on what the teacher wants to achieve. There is an argument that this means lessons are structured by experts who have the overall aims in sight. There is also one to suggest that objectives set by the teacher, and not involving learners, may limit overall learning in that they are *too* focussed on overall goals. Whether and how you share objectives with your learners is a personal choice and it may be that it is something you change according to the lesson and the learners. With this in mind we have included a few strategies you could use in the 'Leveraging Learning Technology' section. What is important is that your lesson is planned with intent, that you know what learning should be taking place and that you are clear on how you will measure it.

Leveraging learning technology

Technology can support teachers in terms of objectives when used to share or record them. One basic example is to simply design a presentation for a lesson where teachers not only create a 'slide' which covers all of the objectives for the lesson, but then a small box on each subsequent slide which lists the objective being addressed by the slide's content. Some more visual presentation tools like Sutori, Prezi or Canva may perhaps allow learners to see the lesson as a journey, where each step is linked to a specific learning outcome.

When sharing objectives, the key is to add variety whilst maintaining familiarity. We may have chosen to share learning objectives with learners in every lesson but we can be creative in how and, sometimes, when we share them. Learning technologies such as word cloud tools (Mentimeter or other word-cloud generators) may be an interesting way to do this. The use of anagram generators or puzzle generators where learners have to solve or decipher the objectives might also be useful.

When learners set their own objectives for a lesson, technology can be of great help in tracking them. Using Excel on Office 365 or Google Sheets can allow you to share a file with learners where they enter their objectives for a workshop or practical session and then reflect on their progress at various points throughout the session. This can also be done with the use of a basic form or questionnaire on Microsoft or Google where the teacher can ask specific questions and their answers will automatically go into a spreadsheet they can track. This strategy can allow teachers to help students create effective objectives and track objectives between sessions and even to sessions taught by other teachers.

Links to the tools mentioned in this section can be accessed via this QR code.

Summary

In this chapter, we have considered the short journey that happens within every lesson and recognised that reaching the ultimate learning destination means knowing where the important landmarks are. Learning aims and objectives help us to pinpoint these landmarks, as well as measure whether or not we have reached them. We have also considered the importance of motivation in any journey we undertake. Any form of travel requires movement; we must be driven to undertake the journey in the first place and recognise that we have the skills needed to arrive safely at our destination.

References

Bloom, B. (1965) *Taxonomy of Educational Objectives: Handbook 1 Cognitive Domain.* London: Longman Higher Education.

Carroll, L. (2021) *Alice's in Wonderland: The Original 1865 Edition with Complete Illustrations By Sir John Tenniel (A Classic Novel of Lewis Carroll).* Great Britain: Amazon.

Dweck, C. (2017) *Mindset.* 6th edition. London: Robinson Publishing.

Jussim, L. and Harber, K. D. (2005) 'Teacher Expectations and Self-fulfilling Prophecies: Knowns and Unknowns, Resolved and Unresolved Controversies', *Personality and Social Psychology Review*, 9(2): 131-155.

Keller, J. (1987) 'Development and Use of the ARCS Model of Instructional Design', *Journal of Instructional Development*, 10(3): 2-10.

Lazowski, R. A. and Hulleman, C. S. (2016) 'Motivation Interventions in Education: A Meta-Analytic Review', *Review of Educational* Research, 86(2): 602-640.

Murdock-Perriera, L. and Sedlacek, Q. (2018) 'Questioning Pygmalion in the Twenty-First Century: The Formation, Transmission, and Attributional Influence of Teacher Expectations', *Social Psychology of Education* 21: 691-707.

Rosenthal, R. and Jacobson, L. (1968) *Pygmalion in the Classroom: Teacher Expectation and Pupils' Intellectual Development.* New York: Holt, Rinehart and Winston.

Rosenthal, R. and Babad, E. Y (1985) 'Pygmalion in the Gymnasium', *Educational Leadership*, 43(1): 36-39.

3 Starting the lesson

Introduction

You will probably have heard the phrase *You will never get a second chance to make a first impression* (attributed to author Andrew Grant), you may have even been told that it takes less than 10 seconds for someone to form an opinion of you. A sobering thought – but not quite as scary as the research evidence. According to Wills and Todorov (2006), it actually takes others less than a second to make these judgements, which suggests that first impressions are very important. As teachers, we have the opportunity to make first impressions on a regular basis, every day in fact. Each time we begin a new lesson we are making a first impression and for this reason we need to start in a positive way. In this chapter we will explore ways of creating a great start to lessons, how to encourage readiness for learning and ways in which we can build on and connect to prior learning.

Readiness for learning

In an ideal world learners would come to lessons highly motivated, having completed any homework assignments and focussed on the task in hand. Whilst desirable, this probably isn't the norm in most classrooms. Learner motivation may be less than ideal for a whole host of reasons and sometimes an individual might simply be having a bad day. All good teachers want to motivate their students, but there is very little you can do about events prior to your lesson. Some students will not be ready to learn, and this can be disconcerting for teachers.

The notion of 'readiness to learn' is based on a number of principles related to learners' abilities to acquire knowledge by actively engaging in the learning process. There may be several factors which impact on this and ultimately influence dispositions towards learning. These include:

- *Physical factors* – the physical environment is important here but this also relates to external factors such as health, hunger and wellness.
- *Emotional readiness* – includes learners feeling a sense of security in the classroom or anxiety around learning and confidence.
- *Experiential readiness* – previous learning experiences such as perceived failures and successes may have influenced self-efficacy in relation to learning.

DOI: 10.4324/9781003385905-4

- *Knowledge readiness* – new knowledge is built on prior knowledge, so if a learner has some gaps or misconceptions these will influence the ability to assimilate new learning.

Learner readiness is a significant factor in how learners are able to engage in lessons in order to absorb and process new information. It is closely connected to motivation in that it explores the barriers that may exist for individuals. When you consider the list of factors we have included in this chapter, it is clear that some are easier for teachers to address than others. The important thing to remember is that teachers do have a significant influence and can positively promote learning readiness, often by making some simple adaptations to their practice.

Reflection

Reflect on your own practice and the ways in which you may have enhanced or diminished learners' readiness to learn, consider any adaptations you have made and perhaps some things you may have missed. You may also consider what the first 5-15 minutes of your session is typically like from the perspective of learners and how you are enticing them to engage in the lesson.

Starting strong

Have you ever thought about teaching as a form of performance art? Our stage is the classroom and our 'performance' the way in which we present the lesson and ourselves. Both have a significant impact on our audience (our learners). A colleague often relays a tale of her own student days which illustrates the importance of starting lessons in a positive way. Her teacher was introducing a new unit of study and began by apologising for the content 'I'm sorry but we have to start unit x ... It's really complex and quite dull.' Her introduction continued by outlining all of the negative aspects of the unit, her language varying from apathy to animus, before cheerfully announcing 'Don't worry, we'll get through it!' Compare this to the teacher who bounces into the classroom, full of enthusiasm for the lesson content, who welcomes the students by telling them all about the exciting adventure they are about to undertake exploring a new subject. Which would you prefer?

The way a lesson starts is often an indicator of its overall success. As the example above shows, a lesson introduction can motivate or de-motivate simply by influencing expectations. Over the past few years there has been a lot of interest in lesson starters – short activities aimed at grabbing the attention of the audience. Premised on the idea of introducing fun into learning, starters often take the form of a challenge or game, are easy to implement and are a great way to engage learners. This is a positive start, but we should add a word of caution ... starter activities are simply an appetiser for the lesson, they are not the main event. It is important that they are relevant to the topic and provide a taste of the overall content but don't dominate.

Making learning fun can be very addictive but remember that although your enthusiasm and demeanour can and will influence your students, your lessons don't have to be theatrical productions. What is important is that they are effectively planned and have a clear structure underpinned by the intended learning outcomes. To do this it is important that learners know what they are doing and why. This means sharing the content of the lesson and showing its relevance to the bigger picture. This idea is simply conceptualised in the 3Is of the inspection framework (Ofsted, 2019): Intent – focussed on the curriculum and intended learning; Implementation – which is concerned with the design of teaching and assessment; and Impact which stresses the importance of learners developing the required knowledge and skills in readiness for the next stage of education. Put simply this could be described as:

- What?
- How?
- So what?

Building on prior learning

As we have shown in the previous anecdote, the start of a lesson can set the tone and environment of what is to follow. If you want learners to be in groups; how can you leverage the starter activity so that learners end up in the groups you need? How might a starter activity control the way learners enter the room so that the lesson has a clear and sharp beginning? Although it is easy to go too far with a starter activity and let your lesson reach a crescendo too early, this is an element of the lesson where creativity in your practice can be unleashed and it is worth remembering that the most creative and effective practice doesn't have to be labour intensive.

According to Rosenshine's (2012) principles of effective instruction, the first element is beginning a lesson by reviewing previous learning. The intention here is to link learning together by making connections and creating a sense of continuity. This approach also helps to build learners' confidence as they review previous learning and a good starter will engage them as soon as they enter the room. Simple tasks can work very well, for example:

- *The big question* – put an open-ended question on the board to spark debate. Perhaps – What is morality? Why do we need electrical regulations? Should hairdressers have training in counselling?
- *Matching/pairing activities* – write questions and answers on separate note cards or post-it notes. Give these to learners as they enter the room and tell them they have to find the answer or question that matches their card.
- *The hook* – have a video already playing on the screen that relates to the topic of the session – the more dramatic the better. Then elicit the objectives from the group by asking them what the lesson is about.
- *The puzzle or mystery* – have a task for the group (or for small groups) to solve when they come in, this could be as simple as a word scramble or cloud containing the lesson objectives all jumbled up. Alternatively, opt for an escape room task where learners have to crack a code to open a luggage lock on a rucksack, that has the objectives inside.

These ideas could be adapted for any lesson – they are simply aimed at grabbing attention and getting learners actively involved from the outset.

Metacognition

A major part of our work as teachers is supporting learning by helping individual students to find strategies to access and assimilate information. As suggested by Dunlosky et al. (2013), many students are not using the most effective strategies to support their learning. The research suggests that students seem to be committed to strategies that have limited impact such as the use of re-reading and highlighting. There may be reasons for this, for example, teachers themselves not being aware of the variation in the effectiveness of different strategies, which in turn means that ineffective strategies may have been reinforced through years of learning. This research also found that greater importance is attached to teaching content and critical thinking, than on the strategies which can guide and promote individual learning. However, the study itself was based on techniques that students could use without supervision or specialist resources, which meant that it excluded a number of digital strategies which have recently become much more commonplace within classroom practice. That said, the findings are still very significant. There remains an emphasis on content above all else, often neglecting the importance of teaching learners how to learn.

Metacognition used to be described as 'thinking about thinking' and at a simple level, that's exactly what it is. But what does it mean in relation to classroom practice? Metacognition really translates into 'self-knowledge' in that it is the knowledge we gain about our mind and how it works. This makes it very powerful as it allows learners to think about what's working (or not) so that they can adapt their approach to get better results. In turn, this provides an opportunity to stop going over and over the same ground and helps move towards achieving their aims. After all, there is little point in spending hours reading, notetaking or highlighting, if that isn't helping to make sense of, or retain, any new knowledge.

Developing metacognition means developing awareness and self-efficacy in relation to learning. When we know what strategies work, we can save time and energy and, more importantly, begin to feel successful in our studies. To do this we need to have an awareness of cognitive processes such as:

- The use of logic and reasoning to solve problems;
- Creating mental imagery of how things might look;
- The use of insight to come up with new ideas;
- Using evaluation to select things which will work best in a given scenario;
- Creativity to generate new ideas;
- Synthesis – combining different elements into a new whole.

All of those things are useful skills in themselves and can easily be built into lesson activities. Table 3.1 includes some simple suggestions related to each of them. The ideas outlined in italics have sample activities which can be found by following the QR link provided.

Table 3.1 Strategies linked to cognitive processes

Logic/problem solving	Simple puzzles related to the topic.
	Group activities such as *the egg drop*.
Creating mental imagery	Use stories to 'paint a picture'.
	Visualisation activities such as *scripted fantasy*.
Developing insight	Journaling to encourage personal reflection.
	Activities which explore personal perceptions and experiences such as the *Roadmap activity*.
Evaluation	Encouraging choice through activities such as *Four Corners*.
	Selecting given solutions to a problem.
Creativity	Building something out of given resources.
	Putting ideas into visual forms using mindmaps, posters or videos.
Synthesis	Paragraph synthesis using different sets of information.
	Case studies outlining issues and previous solutions.

Any number of strategies could be used ... the key is to encourage your learners to think about their learning and in doing so, discover the strategies that work for them.

Avoiding overload

New teachers are usually very keen to teach their learners everything they know – what a wonderful thing that is! However, teaching your students *everything* may not be quite as helpful as it seems – especially when you try to do it in a single lesson. Many of us have done just that as can be illustrated in the following example.

Learn from our experience

This excerpt is taken from an experience of one of the authors, so is written as a personal reflection.

During my teacher training I was blessed with a wonderful group of learners. There were keen, motivated and soaked information up like eager sponges. So much so,

I decided to share as much knowledge as possible with them. They were always so pleased that the lessons were full, and they went away with lots of additional notes. Indeed, they often told me how good my lessons were because I gave them loads of handouts. As for me, I spent most of my weekends planning this single lesson, they absorbed information so easily I seemed to get through a whole semester's worth in a single session. I wasn't worried though, they had been given everything I had, surely they were going to excel when it came to their assessments?

When the time came, I couldn't wait to look at their work. I was expecting detail, well thought out arguments, clear analysis of information ... maybe even some creative thought. What I got was bland, somewhat confused responses which rarely veered from the obvious. The whole group had completed the assignment tasks in the most basic way and mostly using the content from the course textbook.

How disheartening that experience was but what a great lesson it turned out to be. After many painful reflections, I realised that I had simply overwhelmed the group. My enthusiasm and detailed planning were great, but I had forgotten that my learners needed time to absorb the information and to use it for themselves. In essence, I had simply overloaded their short-term memory.

As Cowan (2008) outlines, memory consists of three types, long-term, short-term and working memory, which differ in how they deal with information. What is most important in this example is that the short-term memory has a capacity limit, which means it can only accommodate so much information at once. Cowan (2008, citing Hebb, 1949) likens the short-term memory to a pattern of 'neural firing' linked to a particular idea which is only firing when the idea is active. So, during a class what we have worked on might seem sharp, but when that period of activity ends, so too might the memory. Working memory, whilst not dissimilar, refers to memory used to plan and carry out behaviours. We may remember stages we have already completed in a process. For example, when baking a cake, the working memory stores previous steps and we are likely to remember which ingredients have already been added. Long-term memory differs in two distinct ways, the first is duration of memories and the second is to do with storage capacity. Whilst the long-term memory provides a record of previous events and a store of knowledge (even if this may be incomplete); there is a limit to how many items the short-term memory can hold. In addition, if there is a limit to storage capacity then it is also likely that the introduction of new information may replace what is already stored. A controversial idea perhaps and one which may have inspired Miller's famous 'magical number' theory (1956) which suggested that adult memory capacity handled seven (plus or minus two) things at once. This idea (whilst perhaps oversimplified) does outline an important point, we can hold approximately seven items in our short-term memory at once (even if they are not all separate entities). Therefore, overwhelming students with information may not be all that helpful!

Cognitive load

Cognitive load theory (CLT) considers the factors which can negatively influence learning and is based on a model of how the brain stores and processes information into schemas. We introduced this idea in Chapter 1 so you may remember that a schema is a framework used by the brain to store and categorise information as well as show relationships between things. It could be described as mental architecture which influences our attention to, and subsequent assimilation of, new learning. Schema, whilst helping us to develop our understanding of the world, might also present a block to receiving information which does not 'fit in'.

CLT is based on the idea that the brain can only handle so much information at once and any factors which distract learners will increase the cognitive load, making it more difficult to pay attention and subsequently remember the learning (Sweller, 1988). There are three forms of cognitive load:

- Innate difficulty in a task (intrinsic);
- Demands imposed by others (extraneous);
- The construction of relevant schema to support memory (Germane).

We have all experienced learning moments where the work was so challenging that we just wanted to give up. Sometimes new information seems counterintuitive or just doesn't fit with our worldview, sometimes the language of new learning is so complex it is difficult to see beyond the words and we may not see the immediate relevance of what we are learning. When we experience these intrinsic difficulties, the easiest way to address them is by breaking down information into smaller chunks. Small simple steps to build up to where we need to be.

The example in the 'learn from our experience' section is a clear illustration of extraneous cognitive overload. New teachers often fall into the trap of overloading their students with information and students can be quite complicit in this as very often, they mistake the giving of information with good teaching. In the example provided the overload was the result of too much information which detracted from the key learning, but extraneous overload can also occur when instructions are too complex, so clear presentation of information is key. Too often we see teachers smothering their students with detail when they are explaining a point or directing activities. Whilst done with the best of intentions, one thing we need to remember is that the meaning of our communication is the response we get. It is unlikely that we will diffuse confusion by simply adding more information. Think of it as a Venn diagram, what we say is what *we think* we are communicating, what others hear is *what they think* we are communicating (Figure 3.1). The actual communication is happening somewhere in the middle of the two and that is the area we need to work with. Listening is just as important as speaking so asking questions is vital to ensure that the message we think we have portrayed is actually the same as the one received.

What about germane load? This refers to how we create long-term learning through the construction of schema and involves establishing patterns of thought or behaviour to categorise information. Just like organising your pantry or closet ... if things are stored appropriately, retrieval is a much simpler process and of course the more we retrieve and use information, the more familiar it becomes. There are several things you could do to help

Figure 3.1 Communication Venn diagram

your learners store information in more effective ways, such as the use of mnemonics or rhymes. Some additional examples have been included in Table 3.2

Breaking learning into steps

Cognitive load theory has been used as a tool for instructional design and as discussed is based on the idea that the memory takes the form of schemas which in turn means that processing new information requires some mental effort (Sweller, 2016). An effective way to manage cognitive load is to break learning into smaller steps. This has a dual benefit; first it means you can present things in easily manageable pieces and second that you provide opportunities to review one section of learning before moving on to the next.

Chunking

'Chunking' is a way of grouping information together into more manageable and meaningful pieces and is the premise of good curriculum design. In planning learning we need to think about the intended outcomes as well as how the journey should begin and end, and like any memorable journey there will be twists and turns, steep climbs and easy ambles. If you were planning a long hike, it is doubtful that you would rush from starting point to final destination without any stopping off points. Instead you are likely to plan places to break the journey, perhaps a coffee break or lunch? You might select somewhere beautiful for a picnic or a photo opportunity ... in short, you would plan your journey in a way that makes it memorable.

Table 3.2 Storage strategies

Strategy	Impact
Use a revision task to create a bridge between prior learning and new learning.	This allows learners to make connections and build on prior knowledge – it also gives the impression that new learning is familiar.
Use graphic organisers, flow charts or concept maps to present information.	This helps students to visualise how the new information connects to what they already know.
Keep presentation succinct.	This limits interference from unnecessary information and limits distractions.
Use worked examples to teach specific steps in a process.	This provides a framework for the new learning.
Present verbal and visual information together.	The additional 'clues' make the information easier to process.
Use visualisation techniques to encourage learners to see what they have learnt.	This helps learners to personalise the information to their own preferences.
Get learners to create revision materials such as quizzes, videos or podcasts.	This gives learners an opportunity to consolidate their own learning through synthesis.

By chunking sections of learning we are providing the opportunity to make the learning more memorable. This is done in two key ways – the first is by managing the amount of information presented and the second is finding an easy way to group it together. A typical example of this would be the use of a mnemonic. Most of you will remember the colours of the rainbow, not because you visualised and committed the colours to memory but because you learnt the mnemonic Richard Of York Gave Battle In Vain (or, if you are American, the name Roy G. Biv). A small chunk of information presented in a memorable and meaningful format is much easier to remember than Red, Orange, Yellow, Green, Blue, Indigo, Violet. To translate this to your teaching practice, there are a few principles to remember:

- Information is easier to digest when it is broken into small, organised units.
- Information is easier to understand when the level of detail is correct. This means, appropriate for your audience.
- Information should be limited to a manageable amount – Miller's magic seven principle might provide a useful guide for the number of items in each unit.

When content is presented in smaller chunks it is not only easier to digest it is easier to assess. By breaking down content in this way you create the opportunity to put in place learning checks which in turn will provide you with evidence about how effectively the new information has been absorbed and inform your future planning. It is an effective feedback loop which helps both teachers and students.

Reinforcing learning

When you learn a language, how to ride a bike or how to cut hair, you don't learn the theory and immediately apply it perfectly. Any of these skills require practice, correction, and more practice in a continual cycle until the skill can be carried out with ease. Retrieval practice has become a hot topic in education circles because of the potential impact on learning. Most studies are based on the premise that the simple act of retrieving information from our memory increases our ability to recall it in the future (Carpenter and Delosh, 2005; Carrier and Pashler, 1992). Argawal et al.'s (2016) study takes this one step further by considering the effects for students who varied in working memory capacity. An important finding from their research was that retrieval practice during learning, when accompanied by feedback, has a significant impact on 'lower capacity students'. It is extremely useful to have this confirmed by research, but we are willing to bet that anyone who has been involved in skills-based teaching, would have been able to tell us the same thing

You may have heard of the '10,000 hour rule', which is based on the idea that it takes around 10,000 hours of practice to become highly skilled at something (Gladwell, 2008). It makes sense doesn't it? But when you work that out ... if we are working (or studying) an average 35-hour week for around 48 weeks a year (we all need holidays) – then it would take approximately 6 years to develop the required level of expertise. Whilst the rule itself may be oversimplified, the message is a powerful one. To become skilled at anything, we need to practice. We not only need to learn knowledge, we also need to retrieve and use it regularly.

Developing expertise isn't simply about completing a certain number of practice hours, it involves practising in a very deliberate way and is based on highly structured activities which are created to improve performance as well as providing opportunities for feedback and correction (Ericsson, 2006). When building deliberate practice into your teaching, there are some basic principles to consider:

- Make it systematic – most subjects have specific techniques which are useful in building knowledge and skills, for example in languages 'listen and repeat' is often used to build fluency. Build these elements into your planning.
- Use small steps and a mastery learning approach – practise one aspect of the skill until it is mastered before moving on to the next.
- Make sure practice is guided – this means you need opportunities for formative feedback to modify performance and avoid repeating mistakes.
- Use specific goals to target – try to take an ipsative approach. This means learners should set goals against their own previous performance rather than generic goals that might be set for a whole class.
- Ensure practice is deliberate – in that it requires conscious action and full attention.

Leveraging learning technology

There are a broad range of technologies that are perfectly suited for starter activities, but we are aware that the sheer amount of possibilities can be overwhelming and sometimes it is difficult to know which strategy to use. If you choose to start your lesson by assessing prior learning, you might choose from the broad range of quiz tools available, such as Kahoot, Socrative or Quizizz. What you choose depends on your intention. Socrative and Quizizz are perhaps better if you want to ask different question types which access higher skills such as analysis and synthesis. Quizlet is great for the range of activities you can build and Blooket allows you to create and run all sorts of app-style games around a set of questions. If planning time is the issue, try Sporcle.com, which has millions of quizzes on every topic you can imagine, although beware it does contain advertisements. Another approach is to do an interactive task on the board such as a mind map. In this case Miro, which is an online interactive whiteboard with lots of pre-built mind map templates, is a great option. Alternatively, as suggested earlier, you might want to start with a 'Big Question' or debate – for this Kialo is an excellent tool as it allows learners to formulate arguments and ideas.

We have included some links to these resources – just scan the QR code presented earlier in this chapter and the choices will appear.

Summary

In this chapter we have discussed the importance of creating a positive start to your lessons by supporting learners to engage from the outset. As suggested in the introduction, *first impressions count*, so we need to spend time ensuring we start with a clear focus and in a way that provides learners with the opportunity to reinforce their previous learning at the same time as enabling them to connect it to something new. The suggested strategies take into account the importance of metacognition by considering effective ways of supporting learning, as well as ensuring that we do not overload learners with content. It is a balancing act of course, but remember with each chapter you are polishing your skills and building a repertoire of strategies to call on when you need them.

References

Argawal, P. K., Finley, J. R., Rose, N. S. and Roediger III, H. L. (2016) 'Benefits from Retrieval Practice Are Greater for Students with Lower Working Memory Capacity', *Memory*, 25(6): 764–771. http://dx.doi.org/10.1080/09658211.2016.1220579.

Carpenter, S. K. and Delosh, E. L. (2005) 'Application of the Testing and Spacing Effects to Name Learning', *Applied Cognitive Psychology*, 19: 619–636.

Carrier, M. and Pashler, H. (1992) 'The Influence of Retrieval on Retention', *Memory and Cognition*, 20: 633–642.

Cowan, N. (2008) 'What Are the Differences between Long-Term, Short-Term and Working Memory?', *National Institute of Health*, 169: 323–338. doi:10.1016/S0079-6123(07)00020-9.

Dunlosky, J., Rawson, K. A., Marsh, E. J., Mitchell, J. N. and Willingham, D. T. (2013) 'Improving Students' Learning with Effective Learning Techniques: Promising Directions from Cognitive and Educational Psychology', *Psychological Science in the Public Interest, Association for Psychological Science*, 14(1): 4–58. doi: 10.1177/1529100612453266

Ericsson, K. A. (2006) 'The Influence of Experience and Deliberate Practice on the Development of Superior Expert Performance' in K. A. Ericsson, N. Charness, P. J. Feltovich and R. R. Hoffman (eds), *The Cambridge Handbook of Expertise and Expert Performance*. New York. Cambridge University Press, pp. 683–703.

Gladwell, M. (2008) *Outliers: The Story of Success*. New York. Hachette.

Hebb, D. O. (1949) *Organization of Behavior*. New York: Wiley.

Miller, G. A. (1956) 'The Magical Number 7, Plus or Minus 2: Some Limits on Our Capacity for Processing Information', *Psychological Review*, 63: 81–97

Ofsted, (2019) Education Inspection Framework. Available at: Education Inspection Framework – GOV. UK (www.gov.uk) [Accessed 13 December 2022].

Rosenshine, B. (2012) 'Principles of Instruction: Research Based Strategies That all Teachers Should Know', *American Educator*, 12–39.

Sweller, J. (1988) 'Cognitive Load during Problem Solving: Effects on Learning', *Cognitive Science*, 12: 257–285. doi: 10.1207/s15516709cog1202_4.

Sweller, J. (2016) 'Working Memory, Long-Term Memory and Instructional Design', *Journal of Applied Research in Memory and Cognition*, 5: 360–367.

Wills, J. and Todorov, A. (2006) 'First Impressions: Making Up Your Mind after a 100-MS Exposure to a Face', *Psychological Science*, 17(7): 592–598.

4 Using resources and activities

Introduction

What exactly do we mean by resources and activities? In general they can be viewed as things that facilitate and support learning. The terms are often used together, so much so it is difficult to separate them; resources and activities are like salt and pepper, tea and crumpets, Tarzan and Jane. So entwined we often refer to them as a single entity. So, let's clarify that from the outset; a resource is usually a 'thing', an object (although we will talk about using people as resources … so bear with us on that point) and an activity is something we do in the class. In a nutshell, we use resources to support our planned activities. Teaching resources, and the activities associated with them, are an essential part of classroom practice; the important thing to remember is that the actual *resource* (the thing being used) is significantly less important than *how* it is used. In this chapter we will examine the reasons why this is the case and introduce you to ways in which you can use resources and activities to promote learning.

Stages of learning

There is a reason why the journey metaphor is often applied to learning … it is very rare we jump from A to B, teleported, Dr Who style in a matter of seconds. In most cases we meander along a given route and navigate this with guidance from others, or in the form of a map. Learning tends to be incremental; we reach a certain stage and build on it before reaching the next, but to manage this effectively we need to have a clear idea about how learning takes place. In our description of stages of learning we make reference to some key learning theories and Table 4.1 provides a reminder of these to help you make the connection between stages of learning and the type of resources/activities you might use.

Beginning learning – this stage teaching is likely be associated with the behaviourist school of teaching where the teacher is in control of the lesson and is acting as an instructor. The student is being introduced to a new subject or discipline and resources should enable the teacher to provide information in a format the students can relate to easily. Things that may help at this stage are glossaries of new terminology, worked examples or partly completed activities.

DOI: 10.4324/9781003385905-5

Table 4.1 Key learning theories

Learning theory	Key principles
Behaviourism: Has a focus on external factors which influence behaviour.	Behaviour is a response to external stimuli. Behaviour is learned through conditioning. Behaviour is taught through positive reinforcement and punishment.

What does this look like in a learning environment?

The teacher is instrumental in encouraging and discouraging behaviours and manages this through a system of rewards and sanctions.

Learning follows direct instruction and is supported by repetition.

Learning is observable and measurable. We say learning has taken place when we can measure differences in what learners know or are able to do.

Cognitivism Focusses on the inner workings of the mind and how we process information.	Mental processes such as thinking, making sense, problem-solving and memory are important. Knowledge is seen as mental construction. Sees the mind as a computer – what goes in must be processed.

What does this look like in a learning environment?

The teacher's role is to facilitate the learning process by providing opportunities for mental construction.

Prior learning is taken into account and built upon.

Constructivism Learners construct knowledge at a personal level through interaction and experience.	Learners are active in building their knowledge. Previous knowledge is used as a foundation for new learning. Learning is a social activity; we learn from others as well and our environment.

What does this look like in a learning environment?

Constructivism is based on cognitivist beliefs about learning, so everything in the category above is relevant.

Learning is an active process; learners need to engage with learning material in order to remember it.

Social interaction enhances learning.

Consolidating learning – Teaching at this stage is generally associated with a cognitive approach. The teacher is acting as a guide, and the resources need to reflect the need to aid students in making sense of new information or knowledge by making or indicating links to help students build on what they already know. Graphic organisers such as Venn diagrams, mind maps or concept maps can all help in showing connections.

Exploring learning – at this stage the teaching can be associated with the constructivist approach in which learning is an active, individual process where the teacher acts a facilitator. The resources used here should reflect the need for students to create their own learning and understanding. Using group work to share ideas and develop understanding is useful at this stage and learners could be asked to create something which allows them to explore and consolidate their understanding, for example, a mind map or a poster.

Transformative learning – generally speaking, we refer to this when thinking about older learners (adolescent/adults) as it requires critical reflection to adjust thinking, which in turn may be 'transformational' because it opens up new perspectives. Something that Mezirow (1997) refers to as a change in our 'frame of reference' – how we frame our experiences when we process them. As we learn and grow, we acquire new experiences, values and beliefs which form a lens, or a way of seeing and understanding the world, as well as a way of making sense of it. Learners receiving new information initially try to evaluate this in relation to their existing lenses or frames of reference. However, if the new knowledge disrupts the current frame, then it isn't an easy fit in the learner's existing world view. Mezirow would describe this as a 'disorientating dilemma', which simply means that unexpected information or experiences have challenged previous learning, and in turn provided an opportunity to transform our understandings. Research on transformative learning suggests that disorientating dilemmas help to create awareness of conflicting thoughts and ideas and can lead to a reappraisal of perspectives (Mezirow and Taylor, 2009). By questioning what was 'known' before and examining things from a different perspective, the frame of reference is reshaped, allowing the accommodation of new knowledge and insights.

Transformational learning is usually something associated with more mature learners who are able to critically reflect on their views; however, you could argue that this also happens with very young learners when they accommodate new information, although this is less of a transformation and more of an expansion of knowledge. Again, the teacher is a facilitator, but in this instance their role is similar to that of a mentor, encouraging students to learn new perspectives and question their assumptions.

Activity

Look at each of the different types of learning mentioned above and write down the sort of activity or resource that could be used to promote learning and understanding at each stage of the learning process. For example, you might include 'handouts' for beginning learning or 'research' for exploration.

Choosing and preparing resources and activities

As teachers, we are faced with a myriad of resources and activities for teaching and, helpful as that is, it also presents a huge challenge – which one to choose? A digital one using computers, one which involves the students in doing or making something, one that requires them to work individually or one of the allows them to work in a group? Important choices, because we don't want to waste valuable learning time by selecting something which doesn't do the job – but by being aware of potential pitfalls we can ensure that our resource choices support the intended learning. When resources and activities don't work as we imagined, there are usually simple reasons, such as:

- The accompanying activity is over-complicated.
- Instructions are not clear – we haven't been specific about what to do and how to do it.

- We haven't made the connection between what the learners are doing and what they will learn by doing it.
- The resource is just so much fun to use, learners get carried away and go off task.

What's in it for me?

In our experience learners can be very focussed on outcomes and want to know how they will benefit from whatever you are asking them to do – 'What's in it for me?' (WIFM) is a very real phenomena in the world of education, so we probably need to bear this in mind when we consider our choices, and in doing so, make the connection between the resources and activities we intend to use and the learning outcomes we intend to achieve. In other words, when we choose a resource or activity, we need to think about how it will help move the learners from what they know now to what they need to know. Resources designed and used with a clear outcome in mind are much more likely to be successful in supporting learning and there are two important considerations when planning for a particular group of learners:

- Their current stage of learning (what students already know);
- Their learning need (what needs to be improved and why).

Identifying these things at the outset is essential if we want to achieve our aims, after all, if we don't know where we are, or where we are going, we may well just go around in circles.

Assessing the usefulness of the resource or activity

Once the stage of learning has been established, a sequence of three steps can be implemented to assess suitability of our resources and activities:

- Educational focus;
- Audience and relevance;
- Ease of use.

Educational focus

In assessing the educational focus, we need to think about how resources and activities link to the intended outcomes; this is known as constructive alignment (Biggs, 1996). In constructive alignment, the starting point for planning is the statements which outline what learners will achieve at the end of a unit of study. All teaching, assessment and activities are linked in some way to these statements in order to ensure that teaching is focussed and provides learners with the opportunity to construct their learning effectively.

Audience and relevance

As any good presenter knows, it is important to work with your audience and there are a few things to consider here such as the age group, level and prior experience of the cohort. We should also give thought to cultural appropriateness. Whilst ensuring that teaching and learning resources provide challenging and engaging learning, it is also essential that they do not offend students or the wider community due to their content. Consideration should be given to the visual, literary or educational merits of any material that is planned to be included in addition to the normal checks carried out on the type and complexity of language used and its appropriateness for the level of learning. There are, however, some exceptions to this general rule; for example, if teaching a group of adult students, it may be necessary to introduce a controversial text or activity in order to promote discussion, debate or to promote awareness of particular concepts or constructs. If this is an essential part of teaching and learning, then students should be notified in advance that the resource is to be used and possibly given the option of withdrawing if they wish.

We also need to think about practical elements such as ensuring that what we are using is up-to-date and accurate. This is particularly important when using external resources (such as those you might download from websites). Consider also if there is any sort of bias and whether everyone will be able to complete the planned activity/use the planned resource.

Learn from our experience

This is taken from the experience of one of the authors so is written in first person.

Some time ago I taught a lesson on stereotyping. I was teaching a multi-cultural and multi-ethnic group and was aware that there might be potential to cause offence. In the past I had tried group discussions, written exercises, using videos and a range of practical strategies but none of them had really got the message across so I decided to try something new in this lesson. My idea was based on the premise that all the students had one thing in common – their previous education – they had all been to a primary school in the UK and were now in a secondary school. I engineered each group to ensure there were a mix of cultures and ethnicities in each, gave a couple of pieces of A3 paper and a box of crayons to each group and asked them to draw a primary school teacher. The results were interesting to say the least. Nearly all groups drew a Caucasian female and when the exercise was repeated to ask them to draw a secondary school teacher, this resulted in a drawing of a Caucasian male. At first, I was deflated that this represented the learners' prior experiences, then I realised it was actually a huge success. Despite the mixed groups, the learners had in fact outlined typical stereotypes. They may not have realised this initially but when followed by discussion, the meaning of stereotyping and how it evolves was made very clear.

Reflective activity

Think about a controversial subject that you have had to address in one of your lessons or perhaps one that has come from the learners as part of a discussion. How did you tackle this? How successful was the approach? Could you have taught the subject in a different way?

Ease of use

When talking about 'ease of use', this applies to how easy something is for teachers to incorporate into a lesson and how easy the resource might be for learners to use. Some questions to consider are:

- Are you comfortable with the resources you want to use for a particular activity?
- Have you used them before or do you need a 'try out'?
- Are there any additional preparations to make (such as stationery requirements or equipment)?
- Will all learners be able to use the resource, or will you need to adapt it for some of them?

There is nothing more certain to diminish a teacher's credibility in the eyes of the students than using something they don't fully understand, so if you are not fully conversant with whatever you plan to use, take the time to familiarise yourself. That said, it is important to stretch yourself sometimes, particularly when you want to develop your expertise in using more technical resources, so maybe test out your approach with a group you feel very comfortable with or some willing colleagues. The first time you use something new you could also consider providing additional materials such as support notes.

Digital or traditional?

Back in the day (and it's not so long ago) digital resources didn't exist and teachers had to use more traditional resources, pen and paper, chalkboards or even books! Since the inception of the internet and its integration into the curriculum for schools, colleges and universities, the choice of resources available to teachers is almost limitless. This is great news as it widens the scope for approaches to teaching, but it is also important to remember that resources and activities – digital or traditional – are simply teaching tools designed to promote learning, and both can be equally effective.

Using digital technology can be an excellent way of obtaining a quick and accurate picture of the learning stage of individuals or of an entire group. When used as a diagnostic tool, it can also be a method of gathering reliable information about past achievements or difficulties, which can be used in planning teaching. However, digital resources can also lack the flexibility of more traditional resources or activities because you are working with something created by someone else. Think of a digital resource such as Kahoot or Quizizz as a power sanding tool and imagine that a resource such as a set of cards or dominoes is a hand tool, like a piece of sandpaper. Both can be used in the same way, and both can be effective in achieving the overall aim; however, whilst the digital resource can provide an immediate and accurate overview of the whole group, it may not indicate that a particular student or group of students is struggling or has become disengaged. This is where the analogue resources (such as the cards or dominoes) may be better to get into all of the 'nooks and crannies' of students' understanding. This in turn will provide you with the opportunity to observe the detail of individual progress or difficulties. Each of these tools has a purpose, we just need to find the best fit.

Barriers to using ILT

It is fair to say that there has been a drive towards making more use of digital resources and this filters through to wider influences on our practice such as inspection regimes, management observations and even teacher education. Teachers are encouraged to embrace technology – but what of learners? Do they all welcome technological innovation? Do they all have the basic skills required to access technology in a way that is helpful to their learning? There is evidence that a digital divide still exists; an Ofcom survey conducted during the COVID-19 pandemic found that 9 per cent of households with children did not have access to a laptop, desktop PC or a tablet. This rose to 20 per cent when considering all respondents (Ofcom, 2020). This may be surprising to many teachers, but it is important that we are aware that not all students have access to digital devices, and that even when they do have their own devices, they may have limited data available. Indeed, the same Ofcom survey showed that 11 per cent of respondents did not have access to the internet. The benefits of using technology in the classroom do sometimes have to be balanced against practical barriers, so being aware of this is very important.

Another consideration is that not all learners are 'digital natives' (Prensky, 2001). According to the 2019 Learner Digital Perspectives Survey (ETF, 2019), although 53 per cent of learners said that they do not need extra support using technology, 35 per cent said they do. This is still a large number, and it increases for more mature learners – in this case, those in the 19+ category. From a teaching perspective, it is important that we don't make assumptions about what learners will know when it comes to the use of technology. Many of them will be very comfortable and will probably know far more than you do about some applications, but others will have very specific support needs and if you plan to use a particular resource you may well need to spend some time teaching your class how to use it, before you actually teach the content.

Things to consider when choosing digital resources

When choosing a digital resource to use with learners for the first time, it is very likely you will need extra time to set up, to learn how to sign in and to trouble shoot any small hiccups. No resource is guaranteed to work the first time so it may need a bit of adjustment to sort out any teething problems before you use it again. A period of calm reflection and a bit of creative thinking after a lesson can resolve most snags and small issues such as extra time needed can be included in your plans.

Plans should also include any precise rules of the organisation where you work, which may have specific guidelines in relation to the use of digital technology or devices. Learners may (or may not) be allowed to use their own devices in class, and access to a computer room/suite or a specific set of devices may be needed for the activity. Some organisations have their IT security systems set up to ensure that students cannot access specific sites or apps, so if learners can use their own devices, you may need to ensure they are able to access the ones you want to use. There's a lot to think about but don't let that put you off – the rewards of creating an engaging activity will most certainly outweigh any initial difficulties.

Learn from our experience

This excerpt is taken from an experience of one of the authors, so is written as a personal reflection.

The first time I used a learner response system (an older version of some of the quiz websites discussed in this chapter) I was super-organised and printed all the questions as well as posting them on the board, so that everyone could move at their own pace. Learners engaged in the session well and started working through the task, but as the questions got more difficult, they started to talk and discuss the answers. I was determined to assess their knowledge so kept trying to manage the chatter. The focus of the entire activity then became me trying to keep them quiet and doing the assessment on their own, which took a good deal of energy on my part.

Reflecting on the lesson, I realised that I spent a good deal of time and energy in the class keeping my learners from talking about the course content and debating possible answers to key questions. What a waste! I made the purpose of that task about assessment instead of learning. I planned an activity that created buzz and energy and spent all my energy then quelling that enthusiasm!

When you use a digital resource, make sure you use it in a way that matches your intentions, and remember that this doesn't necessarily mean it has to go according to plan. If learning is happening, but they aren't using the resource as intended, does that really matter? Sometimes we can get very focussed on how we imagine things will work and miss the opportunity to make the most of a 'teachable' moment. Just make sure that learning is taking place and let the rest take care of itself.

Working in groups

Planning the right resources and activities is obviously a critical component of teaching and learning but equally important is the context in which they are used and how they might be employed to foster collaboration within groups. By communicating within groups, individuals can enhance their own knowledge and contribute to others' learning, enabling learners to 'take in' new material, including disparate viewpoints. This process provides scope for the integration, reinterpretation and even transformation of knowledge (Millis, 2002), so that learning is 'produced, not reproduced'. In this way, groups themselves become a resource as they have a purposeful role in enhancing learning.

Generally speaking, this process is referred to as collaborative learning, but this description can be divided into two distinctive forms of groupwork - collaborative and co-operative - the aims and methods of implementation of which are very different.

Figure 4.1 Group work

Collaborative or co-operative learning?

Collaborative and co-operative groupwork has similarities:

- Both are based on the idea of active student engagement;
- Both promote student autonomy and interaction;
- Both help in the retention of information and the development of understanding.

The main difference is that co-operative learning is a more formal method of implementing groupwork as it is led by the teacher, whereas collaborative learning groups are more student led. As self-governing groups, they are frequently used to allow students the autonomy to research a subject as a group and come up with their own solutions to problems.

When we plan co-operative learning activities, we need to consider the make-up of the group, and the particular skills individuals will bring to it. We also need to think about the practicalities of organising the groups. Where there are a large number of students in the class it may be possible to divide the groups evenly into smaller numbers. One way of doing this is by giving each student a number and when they have completed the set task in their original group ask them to circulate to different groups. Students with the same number from each group get together, discuss and compare their findings (see Figure 4.1). In this way not only do students benefit from working together in a small group, they are also able share their learning with members of other groups and through discussion consolidate and extend their understanding of the knowledge/skills that they have gained.

In collaborative learning groups, the emphasis is on the individual. Rather than the teacher taking the lead in engineering the group and its activity, the teacher hands the task to the student group, which is autonomous. The teacher does not monitor progress and will only assist the group if asked. Members of the group are accountable to each other; each is responsible for their own work, but they also have a joint responsibility for planning, organising and monitoring the work of the group, sourcing materials and developing strategies to achieve the task's specified outcomes. The success of collaborative learning lies with individuals working towards a common goal whilst also being personally accountable so it may be more suited to more mature learners who are able to communicate effectively and work as part of a team towards achieving a common goal. Having said that, when we refer to 'mature' learners, we are not necessarily referring to age.

Group work or group hate

We are generally encouraged to believe that working in groups is a good thing and that learners love it, but you might be surprised that this isn't always the case. Many people actively dislike group work and sometimes it is easy to see why. I (Carol) confess, when the flipchart paper and pens come out at a staff development event, I know this signals the start of a group activity and actively seek an exit. I am not the only one apparently. It seems that 'grouphate' is a phenomenon (Burke, 2011).

For most of us, groupwork has been set out as some sort of panacea for teaching and when you consider principles of constructivism, where our aim is to provide opportunities for learners to actively construct their understanding, then it does seem like an attractive option. But is it always the best way? Or is there the potential for misconception or even mishap? I am reminded of observing some colleagues who were employed for the Ministry of Defence and had to instruct officers on how to give commands. In this environment, discussion on style of command is perhaps not the most effective use of time and, given the scenarios in which some commands are required, nor is it the safest! Sometimes, direct instruction is required.

Advantages and disadvantages of group work

Despite the somewhat negative introduction to this section, we are well aware that groupwork has a very definite place in the classroom. Some learners do find it engaging and it provides a range of opportunities for exploring and expanding ideas. Some of the key advantages are:

- A group naturally has more resources than an individual, which means there is the potential to bring more information and ideas to a given task.
- Working with others can enhance creativity, this is particularly helpful in problem solving.
- There is some evidence to suggest that when students work in small groups they learn more of what is taught and are more likely to retain the learning (Barkley, Cross and Major, 2005).
- Group work provides the opportunity for reflection on how we work with others, which in turn helps to develop interpersonal skills.

We should also consider some typical disadvantages, such as:

- Very often one person is quite dominant in the group and others may feel that their contributions are not valued.
- There can be pressure to conform to the majority opinion as most people do not like the conflict that can come with expressing a different view.
- Some people are passengers and see group work as a 'free ride'. This can cause resentment, particularly when linked to formal assessments.

Group dissonance

There are also times when working with others can cause dissonance – a sense of dishar-mony when things don't feel quite as they should. This is particularly true if what we are experiencing within a group makes us question previous understanding or beliefs. Festinger (1957) termed this cognitive dissonance and suggested that in order to restore harmony we might need to:

- Change our attitudes and/or beliefs;
- Acquire new information that helps reduce the dissonance;
- Use internal reasoning and justification to accommodate the dissonance (Thompson, 2022:48).

As these adjustments are at a personal level, they may not be easy to implement within a group, therefore it is important to consider the potential for dissonance within the group so that you have some mitigation strategies. Some things to consider are:

- Size of the group – keeping groups small will mean people are less able to be passengers;
- 'Selling' the benefits of working together;
- Rules of operation – getting learners to think about how they might work together in the most efficient way.

If you decide you want a little more control over the process, you might also decide to engineer the groups to maximise the learning potential. You will of course use your know-ledge of the group as a whole to do this but using Belbin's model there are three group roles which could be adopted (Belbin, 2013). These are outlined in Table 4.2.

It is not always possible for groups to have enough people in them to fulfil all the roles Belbin identifies, but most students will feel confident to undertake multiple roles, for example the resource investigator and specialist roles have synergy as do the team worker and shaper roles and could be carried out by one student. In planning the membership of the group, it is essential that it contains social, thinking and action roles – too many of one type can hinder rather than enhance collaboration and lead to the task not being achieved.

Table 4.2 Belbin's model

Social roles	
Resource investigator	Seeks out and gathers information
Teamworker	Promotes teamwork
Co-ordinator	Manages the process designed to complete the task
Thinking roles	
Plant	Creative problem solver
Monitor/evaluator	Analyses information
Specialist	Has specific relevant knowledge or skills
Action roles	
Shaper	Keeps the team focussed
Implementer	Plans strategy
Completer finisher	Quality control

Once the membership of the group has been decided, the task can be launched. The task, for example, could consist of the whole group being required to read and analyse a number of pre-prepared journal articles, book chapters or websites. Alternatively, a jigsaw activity can be set – this is where each student/group is responsible for researching a section of the material and then teaching it to other members of the group. The teacher now adopts the role of observer, monitoring and assessing group progress and only intervening in the group process when it is essential to support the process.

Leveraging digital technology

As you will notice from previous chapters, we have included a leveraging learning technology section, which provides examples of how digital resources can be used to support different aspects of the lesson and these tools can be accessed via the QR code. There is also an extensive list of resources in the appendix (The ILT A-Z). This goes into a little more detail by providing descriptions alongside a brief review of 'pros' and 'cons' related to each resource.

One struggle that many teachers have is keeping track of account information for so many websites. There are a number of tools that help with this – Google Chrome and Microsoft Edge have password storage capabilities and keychain can be used for Apple devices. The important thing is that you review them and change them with some regularity, particularly if you pay for any of your accounts as they will store your payment details. All of these tools will remind you when your passwords may be at risk. It is also useful to keep a list of tools you use in your planning documentation so that you know where to find the resources if you want to use them again. This can be done in a teacher planner, on a lesson plan or by adding links to resources directly into your scheme of work.

Summary

In this chapter we have scratched the surface of the ways in which resources and activities can be planned to enhance teaching and learning. We have explored the ways in which group work can be used as a teaching strategy and considered how we might teach in a more collaborative way and move away from a more teacher-led approach, to one which enhances learner participation and autonomy.

References

Barkley, E. F., Cross, K. P. and Major, C. H. (2005) *Collaborative Learning Techniques: A Handbook for College Faculty*. San Francisco; Jossey-Bass Publishers.

Belbin, M. (2013) *Management Teams, Why They Succeed or Fail*. Abingdon: Routledge.

Biggs, J. (1996) 'Enhancing Teaching through Constructive Alignment'. *High Education*, 32: 347–364.

Burke, A. (2011) 'Group Work: How to Use Groups Effectively', *The Journal of Effective Teaching*, 11(2): 87–95.

ETF (2019) Learner Digital Perspectives Survey. Available at www.et-foundation.co.uk/wp-content/uploads/2019/06/2019-Learner-Digital-Perspectives-Report.pdf [Accessed 26 May 23].

Festinger, L. (1957) *A Theory of Cognitive Dissonance*. Stanford, CA: Stanford University Press.

Mezirow, J. (1997) *Transformative Dimensions of Adult Learning*. San Francisco, CA: Jossey-Bass.

Mezirow, J. and Taylor, E. (2009) *Transformative Learning in Practice: Insights from Community, Workplace and Higher Education*. San Francisco, CA: Jossey-Bass.

Millis, B. J. (2002) *Enhancing Learning – and More! Through Collaborative Learning*. IDEA Paper 38. The IDEA Center.

Ofcom (2020) Nations and Regions Technology Tracker. [online] Available at: www.ofcom.org.uk/__data/assets/pdf_file/0030/198138/tech-tracker-internet-and-device-access-children-data-tables.pdf [Accessed 19 April 2023].

Pensky, M. (2001) Digital Natives, Digital Immigrants. [online] Available at: www.marcprensky.com/writing/Prensky%20-%20Digital%20Natives,%20Digital%20Immigrants%20-%20Part1.pdf [Accessed 19 April 2023].

Thompson, C. (2022) *Reflective Practice for Professional Development: A Guide for Teachers*. Oxon: Routledge.

5 Adaptive learning

Introduction

When we started to write this chapter, one of us acquired an eight-week-old puppy from a rescue organisation. He was there simply because he was blind, and the breeder couldn't sell him. Most of us had had dogs in their lives before but never had a dog with sight problems. The new adoptive 'parent' already had a dog who had been trained to respond to hand signals, but how could this puppy be trained if he couldn't see hand signals? Iniko (that became his name) simply accepted his 'blindness' – not being able to see, using other ways to navigate the world was his 'normal', but a very different 'normal' to that which his four-legged companion, Wanda, experienced. Apart from being (as was later discovered) very partially sighted, he was a perfectly normal puppy, just one with a difference whose training needed to be adapted to enable him to reach his full potential.

Okay, so working out how to teach a blind puppy is not exactly the same as planning ways to teach students in the classroom, but in many respects the challenges are similar. All students are individuals, learning in different ways, at different speeds and in contexts which depend on their abilities, interests and background knowledge, so planning for learning is definitely a challenge. As teachers we want our students to learn so that they can all reach their full potential, and to do that we may have to adapt our teaching methods to facilitate an individual student's learning, something which has become known as adaptive teaching.

Adaptive teaching is not just differentiation – differentiation is simply making sure that teaching is carried out in ways that allow students to access learning by planning different activities for different groups depending on their attainment levels. In a sense adaptive teaching is a derivative of differentiation. Rather than simply knowing the group needs in terms of their educational requirements, it is more about knowing your individual students, being able to recognise any social, physical or intellectual factors that can act as a barrier to learning, and adapting your teaching strategies to help overcome the barriers or at least to ameliorate them. The challenge of enabling students to learn through planning for adaptive teaching and learning can be daunting, but it can be an exciting, stimulating, rewarding and satisfying experience offering, as it does, the opportunity to practise really creative teaching techniques.

In this chapter the focus is on the need to plan for adaptive teaching and learning, the sort of needs that might be encountered in the student group and how planning for adaptive

DOI: 10.4324/9781003385905-6

teaching can benefit not only students with specific needs but *all* students. The strategies for working with students with identified 'special educational needs' (SEN students) are also discussed.

Who do you need to plan for?

Before planning for adaptive teaching can begin, challenges students might be experiencing need to be highlighted. Regrettably, in this imperfect world these are not always something known at the start of a term or even sometimes at the start of a lesson; students' barriers to learning which create the need for adaptive strategies are frequently identified during the process of teaching. Roughly speaking, students' barriers to learning can be divided into two main groups – overt needs, those which are formally identified, and covert needs, the ones that are identified through ongoing informal assessment.

Overt needs

At the start of a year or when beginning to work with a new group of students, teachers will (hopefully) be provided with some basic information in one of two main forms:

- Internally gathered information such as reports, recommendations, lists of exam results, etc. from previous educational establishments.
- Externally gathered information collated from a formal assessment of an individual's educational needs. This may be expressed in the form of an Education, Health and Care Plan (EHCP), which details an individual's needs. Identified needs take a variety of forms but are categorised under four main headings:
  - Communication and interaction;
  - Cognition and learning;
  - Behavioural, emotional, and mental health difficulties;
  - Sensory and/or physical.

Externally gathered information is normally accompanied by guidance on the way(s) in which the need should be addressed. The level of detail in the guidance can vary significantly ranging from general advice about meeting the student's needs in the classroom, to unambiguous recommendations requiring the new educational provider to provide a specific type of support. For example, an EHCP may state a requirement for bespoke additional support in the classroom in the form of a Learning Support or Teaching Assistant (LSA/TA) or a dyslexia diagnosis may require class notes to be presented in a particular format. Whatever the level of detail about the needs of individuals, if the information is available, it is essential it is noted and incorporated in lesson planning. An example of how this might work in practice comes from an experience related by one of our colleagues who recalls how materials were adapted to support a student with a sight impairment. The student was required to access materials from the setting's intranet but couldn't read them. The staff found a simple solution to this – by converting PowerPoints and other materials to Word documents, the learner could use an optical scan reader pen, which would read the information for her.

Covert needs

Covert needs are those which are identified as a result of the teaching process. This is a large group of needs which may manifest at almost any time in observable behaviours which can disrupt teaching and learning. These might include flashes of anger, fear, sadness, lack of interest or sudden displays of hopelessness. Inevitably this can be quite disconcerting for teachers as they may assume they have done something to cause the behaviour, and it is very easy for the sense of hopelessness to be transferred to other students who may be struggling for some reason. When presented with these behaviours it is important to be able to reflect, rather than react – even 'on-the-spot' reflection can lead to helpful adaptations. However, it may be more appropriate to take time to consider the lesson after the event when reflection may result in changes being made to subsequent lessons.

Unlike the overt needs, covert needs are generally those which you spot when you are teaching, and there may be many underlying reasons for them. It is possible that they are the result of short or long-term mental health issues, in which case you need to consider the limits of your role and think about how you might work with additional services to get professional support. Alternatively, anxieties may be short-term responses based on a learner's previous experience. For example, students new to a group who have previously struggled with a subject (maths and/or English being primary examples of this) may disguise negative feelings or difficulties with the subject, by 'acting out' in some way. Covert needs may present themselves in the form of disruption, but these needs are common and can frequently be ameliorated or even avoided by adaptive planning.

To return to our opening paragraph, Iniko's needs were obvious and had been identified by the rescue centre who had made suggestions to help plan and support his progress. However, identifying his covert needs was more challenging, occurring only as his progress towards specific goals was monitored and assessed, just as teachers assess and adapt plans for teaching and learning when working with students.

Starting to plan for teaching and learning

Kipling' 'Six honest serving men' can be a useful tool in developing a lesson plan as they prompt thinking about key aspects:

- *What* you intend to achieve (the lesson objectives);
- *Why* the students need to know the information;
- *When* you're going to teach;
- *How* you intend to teach;
- *Where* the lesson will be (in a classroom, workshop, etc.);
- *Who* is going to learn (the student group).

Of these, five elements are generally included in the plan of work for the subject, but one, and probably the most difficult one, is how you intend to present the information to your learners.

A note about 'learning styles'

At one stage in the not too dim and distant past, one thing teachers were expected to plan for was meeting the 'learning styles' of students – a theory which rested almost exclusively on the notion that students had an identifiable tendency to accept and retain subject matter if it was presented in a particular way. Having identified a specific style of learning, usually through a test of some sort, teachers were expected to plan lessons in a way that met every style to maximise individual learning. We even recall observing lessons where you would be presented with a list of each student's learning style and shown which specific lesson activities had been planned to meet them. Imagine the time that took to put together … and we wonder how often teachers consulted this document during the lesson or whether they simply (and sensibly) responded to the ways students presented to them?

Various theories about the type and number of different 'learning styles' were hotly debated in educational circles. Fleming (2001) suggested that students learnt in one of four ways: visually (seeing something, i.e. video), auditorily (listening to explanations), through reading/writing (taking and making notes, etc.) or kinaesthetically (learning through doing). Honey and Mumford (1992) basing their work on that of Kolb's (1984) experiential learning cycle, suggested that a style of learning could be divided according to type … so we had activists (who liked to learn by doing), reflectors (learnt by reflecting or thinking), theorists (who apparently liked to wrestle with abstract concepts) and pragmatists (who want to try things out). Gardner (2006) in his theory of multiple intelligences suggested that the learning styles were one of eight different forms of 'intelligence': linguistic, logical/mathematical, spatial, bodily/kinaesthetic, musical, interpersonal, intrapersonal and naturalistic. We could go on but suspect you might be confused enough already.

Although the idea that every student has a dominant learning style and that teaching should cater to that style in order to maximise learning has been debunked (Pashler et al 2008; Willingham, 2010; Coffield, 2012) the general concept does retain some merit. Now, before you hold your hands up in horror – we are not suggesting you test learning styles and promptly attach labels to your students. The merit lies in the fact that when we acknowledge that individuals learn in different ways, we must also accept that teaching must be adaptive. If we need evidence of this, we need only look at the different approaches people take to building a self-assembly kit; some will read instructions, others follow diagrams and others throw the paperwork away and just start attaching the various parts until they fit together. Everyone has the same aim but takes a different approach. In the same way, individuals approach learning in ways that best suit them, and as teachers we can facilitate this by adapting our planning to meet some of these preferences. However, we should also consider that a 'learning style' is simply a preference; we can all learn in a variety of ways, therefore, encouraging learners to try out other approaches is something we should plan for.

It is important to remember that learners, as well as teachers, need to be able to adapt to a variety of situations, and if we have learnt anything in the past few years it has been this! The Covid pandemic brought with it the emergence of online lessons which were far from the more traditional methods we were used to. Teachers who previously saw themselves as taking a 'student-centred' approach were suddenly faced with the prospect of talking to a screen when students opted not to use their cameras or interact in the same way as they would in the classroom. Inevitably this led to taking a more 'teaching by talking' approach, akin to traditional lectures. To move away from this, teachers had to adapt. We had no choice but to embrace the change, use technology effectively and find ways to encourage interaction.

Learning from our experience

This reflection is taken from our individual experiences and is written in the first person.

I always endeavour to make my resources attractive and engaging. For me, that means bright and colourful, aesthetically pleasing (in my view, anyway). Preparing resources is something I enjoy so I tend to plan ahead, and on this occasion I had prepared a range of presentations and activities for a series of lessons with my adult learners. During the first lesson, I noticed that one learner seemed to be uncomfortable; he was fidgety and having problems engaging with the topic. At the end of the class he approached me to say that due to a visual impairment, he found dark text on a light background difficult to see. In my view, I had done everything I could to make my resources engaging – it simply hadn't occurred to me that I had in fact created a barrier for one of my learners.

On reflection, this seems quite obvious, but at the time I was so focussed on how the resources looked, I didn't even consider how accessible they might be. With the learner's help, I adapted all my materials and learnt a very important lesson about involving my learners in planning my lessons. It is now second nature for me to 'check in' with learners at regular intervals to ensure that what I am doing is not only engaging but also accessible.

Kolb and 4 Ps

Almost anyone who has ever studied to be a teacher will have come across the work of Kolb (1984) and will have (consciously or subconsciously) integrated his four-stage experiential learning or reflective cycle into their planning. An overview of this has been provided in Figure 5.1.

Kolb's theory shows the stages of the learning process that the student encounters as they assimilate new knowledge or skills, but it has been subject to criticism as it doesn't look at the barriers to learning encountered by students, and it gives no indication as to how teachers can support the students to move from one stage to another. To support this transition, teachers need to introduce the 4 Ps, Perspective, Patience, Persistence and Practice, into the mix.

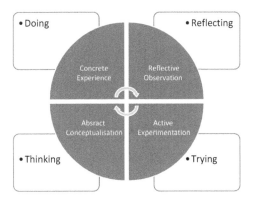

Figure 5.1 Kolb's cycle

Perspective

Assessing the available information on the students, the subject and the existing level of knowledge, provides a 'big picture' or perspective on how the lesson needs to be planned to introduce new learning effectively. Students can be disconcerted by uncertainty about what they will be doing and what will be expected of them. However, some of the 'fear factor' associated with new learning can be lessened by effective planning. For example, introducing an 'advance organiser' (Ausubel, 1960) - a concept map, diagram or other type of visual organiser at the start of the lesson shows learners the shape and scope of the learning journey to come. As students are preparing to move from one stage of the learning cycle to the next, a mini organiser can be used to map out the transition. This not only allows learners to see where they are going, it shows them what they have learned and may promote reflection on which to build further knowledge or skills.

Patience

Patience with students is something which all teachers need. It's a very lucky teacher who hasn't at some point in their career, heard a student say 'I just don't get it' or 'I still don't understand'. Whilst the student may feel that they are simply being 'dumb' what they really mean is that they do not understand the explanation that you have given. Because students access knowledge or skills in different ways, some will need extra support in order to build on what they already know. This is the point at which teaching and learning strategies have to be adapted. By employing a range of alternative strategies and by involving students in the process of providing support, it is possible to clarify concepts and reduce anxiety.

Persistence

By being patient and introducing different strategies you are already exercising the third P - Persistence, but to be persistent you first need to know what to persist with. Finding out where the weaknesses are is done mainly through assessment. The assessment may be formal - marking a piece of written work or a test paper, etc. - but is more frequently informal, taking place in the moment. Gentle questioning can be the first step in identifying the problem; however, a more effective alternative may be to ask the whole group questions to provide you with a guide to any difficulties being experienced as well as avoiding embarrassing or undermining the confidence of an individual. The next step is changing the presentation of the information, giving the same information in a different format, and then checking in again with the students, but it may be necessary to do this several times to enable students to make connections between new and existing knowledge. Persistently reviewing and presenting the subject matter in different ways helps students to assimilate learning through reflection so that they can progress to the next stage with confidence.

Practice

Practice, as the saying goes, makes perfect. Introducing practice at any stage of the learning cycle provides useful feedback on the current level of knowledge and understanding. Practical assessment allows the teacher to identify areas of incomplete understanding, and patiently and persistently adapt their teaching strategies to reprise the salient material. Assessment through questioning is a common practice; however, to assess student progress effectively affirmative questions (those expecting a yes or no answer) or rhetorical questions (those where no answer is expected) should be avoided. Questions must offer the appropriate level of challenge to students but must also be answerable and based on information already given. Questioning encourages students to make connections between different parts of learning so that they can assimilate new knowledge by linking it to what they already know.

Planning for teaching 'special needs'

The term 'special needs' is somewhat contentious. After all, because of our different lived experiences, we all have some sort of special need and, if that is the case, is it really helpful to apply labels? Both Goffman (1963) and Becker (1973) identified the negative effects of applying labels to individuals or groups in terms of both the individual's self-perception and perception of others, which can in turn lead to discrimination. It is difficult for teachers who have been informed that a student has 'special needs' to avoid 'teaching to the label', especially when they have received information about the likely adaptations that will be needed to encourage student success. A 'special needs' student is simply an individual who has a physical or psychological difference of some sort. The needs can generally be planned for and it's much easier to avoid accidental discrimination if the term 'additional needs' rather than 'special needs' is used in a teaching context. However, when we do have learners highlighted with additional needs, we do need to take this into consideration.

Communication and interaction

Using adaptive teaching strategies in terms of communication and interaction is something which can benefit all students. Although communication needs will vary from student to student in general the strategies which fall under the heading of multi-sensory teaching (using visual, auditory and tactile methods) will assist everyone's learning. Modifying 'teacher talk' by avoiding wordy explanations, using simpler less ambiguous sentences, re-stating key concepts, including videos, images and mind maps will help students process information, as will planning in time for students to reflect on new concepts or ideas. Using technology can also improve communication and a vast range of assistive technology such as coloured backgrounds, text-to-speech readers and speech-to-text writing programmes are all available and included in most software packages which can be accessed by all students. Additional support in terms of communication and interaction can also be facilitated by planning for students to work together in small groups.

Cognition and learning

Students with additional needs may take time to absorb new concepts and knowledge but again, many of the teaching approaches employed to assist these students can benefit all students. Pre-teaching new vocabulary and using planners or writing frames are things you can use with whole groups. Demonstrations, practical activities, collaborative working and prompt supportive, constructive feedback will help students retain new knowledge or skills.

Behavioural, emotional and mental health difficulties

For learners who have difficulty understanding and regulating their emotions, a calm, welcoming classroom will go a long way to alleviating some of the challenges they experience. Providing a consistent structure to lessons and starting with easy and familiar tasks may well help to avoid common disruptive behaviours such as acting out or withdrawing. Familiarity and creating a sense of achievement can help learners to relax before you introduce more complex or challenging work, but where appropriate allowing 'time-outs' for students who become stressed or uncooperative provides space for them to think about their responses.

Sensory and/or physical

Sensory processing is simply the way that the brain sorts out information from the environment received via the senses. There are many issues linked to this, ranging from a sensory impairment such as visual or hearing difficulty, to problems experienced with taste, touch or smell. Physical difficulties again are on a spectrum but are more likely to be noticeable and possibly supported using physical aids of some sort. The impact of sensory or physical challenges on an individual are specific and too wide ranging to be summarised here but whatever the effect on the individual it is essential that any available guidelines are incorporated within the lesson plan.

Leveraging learning technology

One of the key elements of using technology in teaching and learning is getting feedback from learners and responding to it. Learners know best what works for them and what doesn't, so getting feedback as you try new tools will be the most effective method of guiding your future choices. Don't be afraid to ask your learners what they think. You could even use technology to do this ... Microsoft or Google Forms would work well for this type of activity.

If you need to adapt your teaching to support overt needs, technology can be really helpful. All mobile devices now come with built-in screen readers and Google and Microsoft classroom tools also have this facility. There are some really good colour overlay apps which learners can use on their own devices (Tintvision for Android phones/tablets and Dyslexia Glasses/Dyslexia browser for Apple) or on a PC (Colorveil) can put an overlay of any colour over anything on the screen. Colorveil is even available as a portable app, which means it can be run off a memory stick on any computer (some systems may restrict this).

The most adaptive resources are those which are most flexible or even allow learners to build their own learning materials, so although we have mentioned it several times, Padlet is perhaps the most versatile and flexible resource. Teachers can easily add video, audio, documents and links to other websites to build inclusive content that presents information in a variety of formats. Wakelet (Wakelet.com) is a similar tool which will allow for similar outcomes.

There are also some interesting presentation tools, which are well suited to adaptive teaching. Nearpod (nearpod.com) is very helpful (but be aware some features are behind a paywall) as it allows you to easily embed a broad range of media and assessment tools right into the presentation, which can be live on the board and beamed to student devices or used for remote learning. Blendspace (blendspace.com) is another tool that is good for multi-modal presentation. Blendspace allows teachers to add presentations, worksheets, videos and quizzes to a tiled display and arrange them in the order they want students to see them.

Of course there are many other options out there, so explore the companion Padlet page for links to all of the tools discussed here. The QR code will take you there.

Working with classroom support

Working with students who have been identified as having additional needs (the overt needs described above) or who have an EHCP may require a team effort with teachers and learning support staff as key players. As a team, there is the potential to provide a strong scaffold of support which helps individuals to build their own strategies in relation to learning. In an ideal scenario, this is exactly what should happen, but often the way that teachers and support staff work together is something which is given minimal consideration. Evidence from the Education Endowment Foundation (Sharples, Webster and Blatchford, 2015) suggests that typical deployment of support staff often doesn't lead to improvements in academic outcomes, nor does it support the development of soft skills, such as motivation, autonomy and approaches to learning. In fact, it may even do the opposite by increasing dependency. That said, the report also noted some positive impacts such as:

- Freeing up teachers time by delegating routine administrative tasks;
- Reducing teachers' workloads and improving their perceptions of stress and job satisfaction.

Indeed, teachers were largely positive about the contribution of LSAs and TAs, recognising their impact on learners who seemed to struggle within class, as well as supporting teachers in maintaining attention and minimising disruption to teaching. Key findings in the report state that support staff spend the majority of their time in informal instructional roles, with a focus on task completion rather than developing understanding and that there is often little time for liaison with teachers. It is not surprising then that the impact on academic outcomes is limited.

Whilst it seems obvious that teachers and learning support should work closely together, the evidence suggests that this isn't always the case, yet there are many simple strategies which can be employed to strengthen this relationship. For example, sharing information about learners' behaviours or reactions, making any specific guidelines accessible, discussing planning and lesson activities. Unfortunately, communication between teachers and LSA/TAs can be ad hoc and takes place during lesson changeovers, which means that support staff often have to go into the lesson 'blind' and try to tune in to what the teacher is doing. By making time to talk, this issue can be overcome.

Working effectively together

In order to change how teachers and learning support staff work together, it is important to remember the differences in roles – teachers are there to teach and LSA/TAs are there to support. Obvious we know, but as the evidence suggests, this division is not always clear. Support staff should not be used as informal teaching resources; they are there to add value to what teachers do, not to replace them. In order to add value, it is important that everyone is fully prepared and knows what to expect in a lesson, so time to share planning is essential. In addition, there are three other strategies which you may find effective:

- *Add value through teamwork* – make your TA or LSA more visible during whole group activities. Maybe they could be the scribe, writing learners' answers on the board, or possibly demonstrate how to use a piece of equipment? Perhaps you could use a carousel approach and each work with different groups? There are many options, the important thing is that you are working together, rather than as separate entities. You could even try using teaching triage whereby the role is to roam the classroom in order to identify learners who may need further help, then flagging this to the teacher.
- *Develop confident learners* – as previously stated, one danger with providing additional support is that this can become a crutch and it is important to encourage learners to take responsibility for their own learning. One way to do this is to create a framework which encourages learners to self-scaffold; this is where the role of the LSA or TA is simply to observe and give time for processing ideas, rather than immediately correcting or completing tasks with (or even for) the learners. The model in Figure 5.2

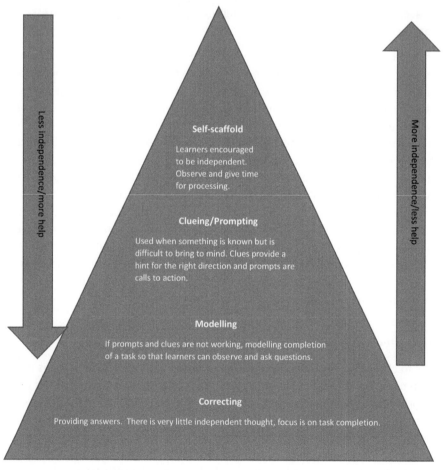

Figure 5.2 The level of support moving from quite direct intervention to something much less directive

shows how this might work in practice with the level of support moving from quite direct intervention to something much less directive.

- One thing you could consider when you begin working with an LSA or TA is contracting. By this we simply mean discussing how your roles work together and reaching an agreement about how your roles can be co-ordinated and differentiated to best effect.

Learning from our experiences

This excerpt is taken from the experience of one of the authors so is written in first person.

Some time ago I did some research on the way TAs could support learning, interviewing both TAs and teachers. The following is taken from one of the interviews following a lesson:

The teacher said:

I really don't know what my TA was up to today – he doesn't seem to have any idea what he is supposed to do. His job is to support one learner – support him, help him to complete his work, guide him through it, explain things to him – not do the work for him. We need to have words!

The TA said:

I'm not sure what I'm supposed to be doing. My line manager says I'm to help the student complete his work, but the teacher doesn't tell me what the work is or where the student's up to. I know what his difficulties are in general – my line manager told me – but he seems to struggle with this lesson more than the others. I'm not familiar with the subject and I'm getting stressed out trying to keep up with the lesson. I need to understand some of it before I can help my student so all I can do is work alongside him so that we (I) can keep up.

Whilst there appears to be a broad gulf between the two in terms of how the TA should be supporting the student, there are at least two points that they agreed on:

- The student needs support from the TA.
- The current support is not working effectively.

To ensure that LSA/TAs work effectively with students it is vital that they are seen as part of the teaching team. If everyone knows what is planned for a lesson, and what their role in implementing the lesson is, there is more likely to be a positive impact. This means three things have to happen:

- Planning should be shared before the lesson so that the TA is conversant with the content.
- The role the LSA or TA will take, the level and type of support that should be given needs to be discussed.

- The requirements for any specific intervention that may be needed as part of the lesson should be outlined.

Both the teacher and LSA/TA's want to work in the best interests of the student so that they can achieve their full potential. These three elements are the basis of an ongoing 'contract' to support the student which can be informally agreed between the teacher and the TA. By the way – the 'contract' needs to be reviewed and updated regularly to ensure that any changes in the student's needs are met. Working effectively with LSA/TAs isn't rocket science, just plain old communication between, and respect for, the work of colleagues.

Summary

In this chapter, we have considered the importance of adaptability and discussed how we might plan an effective lesson for all learners by taking into account overt and covert needs and supporting learners through the 4 Ps (Perspective, Patience, Persistence and Practice). The ways in which the contentious term special needs is applied in educational settings is discussed together with some suggestions about how learners categorised in this way can be supported and how we might work more effectively with additional support staff in order to achieve the most positive outcomes.

References

Ausubel, D. P. (1960) 'The Use of Advance Organizers in the Learning and Retention of Meaningful Verbal Material', *Journal of Educational Psychology*, 51(5), 267–272. https://doi.org/10.1037/h0046669.

Becker, H. (1973) [1963] *Outsiders*. New York: Free Press.

Coffield, F. (2012) 'Learning Styles: Unreliable, Invalid and Impractical and Yet Still Widely Used' in Philip Adey and Justin Dillon (eds), *Bad Education: Debunking Myths in Education*. Maidenhead, UK; New York: Open University Press, pp. 215–230.

Education Endowment Foundation (2015) 'Making the Best Use of Teaching Assistants'. Available at: TA_Guidance_Report_MakingBestUseOfTeachingAssistants-Printable.pdf (educationendowmentfoundation.org.uk) [Accessed 2 June 2023].

Fleming, N. D. (2001) *Teaching and Learning Styles: VARK Strategies*. Christchurch, NZ: Neil Fleming.

Gardner, H. (2006) *Multiple Intelligences: New Horizons in Theory and Practice*. New York: Perseus Books.

Goffman, E. (1963) *Stigma: Notes on the Management of Spoiled Identity*. Englewood Cliffs, NY: Prentice-Hall.

Honey, P. and Mumford, A. (1992) *The Manual of Learning Styles*. Maidenhead: Peter Honey.

Kolb, D. (1984) *Experiential Learning: Experience As The Source Of Learning And Development*. Englewood Cliffs, NY: Prentice-Hall.

Pashler, H., McDaniel, M., Rohrer, D. and Bjork, R. (2008) 'Learning Styles', *Psychological Science in the Public Interest*, 9(3), 105–119.

Sharples, J., Webster, R. and Blatchford, P. (2015) 'Making the Best Use of Teaching Assistants', Guidance Report. *Education Endowment Foundation*. Available at: TA_Guidance_Report_MakingBestUseOfTeachingAssistants-Printable_2021-11-02-162019_wsqd.pdf (d2tic4wvo1iusb.cloudfront.net) [Accessed 28 May 23].

Willingham, D. T. (2010) 'The Myth of Learning Styles', *Change*, 42(5), 32–35.

6 Checking learning

Introduction

A former colleague used to say 'there is no teaching without assessment'. At the time it seemed like a bold statement – surely there is much more to the role? What about planning and creating resources? Teaching activities? Generating a sense of adventure? It seemed he was somewhat limited in his judgement. Assessment is important of course, but is it really the basis of teaching? Sometime later, we realised he was talking about assessment in its widest sense, not simply the end of study activities used to evidence achievement. What he meant was that without regular informal assessment such as questions or in-class tasks, teachers would not have information about what and how their students were learning, so they wouldn't be able to fully prepare for teaching. After all, how do you know what to teach, if you don't know what your students have learnt?

Our inspiration for this (the late James Atherton) was probably basing his comments on the work of Paulo Freire, who made very clear the connections between teaching and learning by saying: 'Whoever teaches learns in the act of teaching, and whoever learns teaches in the act of learning' (Freire, 1998:31). Freire was well aware of the connections between teaching and learning, and recognised that education could be ideological – not always in a good way. Ideology can lead to passion for the job and an endless search for knowledge. It can also lead to dogma! Freire's belief was that teaching requires the ability to be critical and the humility to recognise when we are wrong. Here is where the link to assessment lies. By incorporating regular, formative assessment, we not only have more information about what our students have learnt, we also have a sense of what *we* need to do differently. This is the foundation of good teaching ... so it seems our esteemed colleague was right all along! In this chapter, we will explore ways of using assessment as a foundation for practice and a vehicle for improving our teaching and our students' learning.

Basic principles of assessment

Assessment is both a measure of what has been taught and what has been learnt. It can be formal or informal and takes place in numerous different ways. Many of these will already be familiar to you – if we asked you to list some strategies you could probably name at least ten things, for example, examinations, essays and practical assessments. We are certainly

DOI: 10.4324/9781003385905-7

familiar with the assessments we have experienced as learners but very often, when we think about assessment, this becomes our focus. Memories of examination stress, assessment anxiety when we await the results of an essay submission and the sheer terror of having to carry out a practical task in front of an assessor! Alternatively, the excitement and warm glow we get from positive, constructive feedback can stimulate the drive to read and learn even more and the sheer challenge of pulling off your best performance. Whichever way you react to assessment, it is sure to be attached to some form of emotional response. But it isn't just the big events we should focus on. Informal assessment is a very natural part of the interaction between students and teachers, so much so, we sometimes take it for granted and don't realise the impact it can have on the overall effectiveness of our teaching. Exam results are important, of course, but we would argue it is the day-to-day assessment activity that really makes the difference.

We are likely to use informal and formal assessment to diagnose specific learning needs at the beginning of a course, or to identify misconceptions or gaps in learning. We also use it to evaluate teaching, so in one way or another it is with us from the beginning to the very end of the learning process. For this reason, we need to ensure that it is carried out reliably and fairly and that means having a clear understanding of some of the key principles relating to assessment.

Types of assessment

Although our focus here is about the use of assessment to check and enhance learning, it is important to note the other ways in which assessment activity is used. When we talk about assessment, we are usually referring to three things:

Formative assessment refers to the assessment activities undertaken by teachers (and learners) which provide feedback on progress. This is subsequently used to adapt teaching and in turn improve learning. When used skilfully, formative assessment, which includes constructive feedback (often referred to as assessment for learning) can have the effect of improving the performance of students as well as motivating them (Speckesser et al., 2018). This is the type of informal assessment we referred to in the introduction; those day-to-day activities such as questioning or 'knowledge-checks' that are embedded into every lesson. Formative assessment provides an opportunity for two-way communication and helps to identify specific areas for development, something which is essential if we want to create an inclusive learning environment. However, it should come with a word of warning. Whilst this type of assessment is often heralded as the cornerstone of learning development, it isn't always carried out effectively. We have seen many lessons where assessments are used as a way of varying teaching activities. When this happens, they simply become additional tasks with no real purpose or benefit. For formative assessment to be useful, it needs to be purposeful. As outlined by Black and William (1998), assessment becomes formative when the evidence is used to adapt teaching and to direct learning.

Closely linked to this is *ipsative assessment* in which individual learners are compared against their previous performance rather than a set of criteria. This is a way of personalising learning and is often used in conjunction with setting individual targets. This level of personalisation is more likely to help learners to act on any feedback they have been given. It also helps to build confidence as they can see their progress as well as the clear plan they have in place to make further improvements.

The third, and perhaps most well-known form of checking learning is the *summative assessment*. This refers to the process of judging achievement in relation to course aims, or criteria set out by the bodies who award qualifications. Many of us associate this with traditional forms of assessment such as examinations or written work, but of course there could be a whole range of assessment activities involved. The important difference is that these will be formal activities which are aligned to the assessment criteria outlined within qualifications. Summative assessments are important ... they are the stuff of judgement. We pass or we fail. We are graded in the top percentile – or we scrape by. This may be a sign of how much we have learnt – or it may evidence how good we are at completing assessments. For both teachers and learners, summative assessments are an emotive topic and for this reason they often become the primary focus. In addition, the data resulting from them can become a managerial tool used to judge teachers as well as learners. As suggested by Black and William (1998), this has led to a situation where the grading function is over-emphasised, whilst the giving of useful advice in relation to learning is not given enough emphasis.

Addressing misconceptions and closing gaps

Through our life experiences we develop naive theories about everything we encounter (Savion, 2009) and given that most of this happens before we receive the guidance that accompanies a formal education, it is inevitable that we will make a few shortcuts when constructing our understanding. This might take the form of jumping to conclusions or assigning the label of 'truth' to a particular assumption, even in the event of coming across conflicting information. Savion refers to this as 'belief perseverance', a state of mind which motivates us to avoid or discredit information that may conflict with our naive understanding of something, even if that understanding is based on a misconception. 'Not an issue' you might say ... 'I will simply make sure I am clear about what is correct and what is not so that my learners are not confused'. But therein lies the problem.

Unlearning theories and principles we have previously absorbed is not an easy process. To illustrate this we need only consider Festinger's work on cognitive dissonance, which we introduced in Chapter 4. This is based on the idea that in order to maintain a sense of equilibrium, we will hold on to current beliefs and assumptions in the face of conflicting evidence as this 'feels' more comfortable than acknowledging that our beliefs were wrong (Festinger, 1957). To do this we might create acceptable reasons to discredit the new evidence, that way we can validate our original beliefs. Festinger provides an example of this in a story about a small religious group whose leader had predicted that the world would end as a result of a flood. The followers were provided with detail about a specific day for this event and told that only the faithful would be saved. In preparation, people left their jobs and got rid of their possessions. When the flood did not take place on the designated day their response was not to question this initial wisdom but to become more devoted to their

leader! In order to achieve equilibrium, they simply found ways assimilating the new information whilst holding on to their beliefs.

For teachers, it is important to know that misconceptions are probably the norm rather
than the exception. They are a part of the learning process and may be formed as a result
of exposure to incorrect or incomplete information, flawed reasoning or misinterpret-
ation of the information they are presented with. Whenever we learn something new we
are likely to use our previous knowledge to help us make sense of the new learning, but if
the prior knowledge is based on misconceptions then the likelihood of misunderstanding or
misinterpreting the new information is much higher. Misconceptions abound in all areas of
life, as an example we have highlighted some of the more common ones you may have come
across in Figure 6.1.

Food must be eaten by its 'best before' date (actually most properly stored foods can
safely be eaten well past these dates).

In the Middle Ages, spices were used to mask the flavour of rotting meat before
refrigeration (spices were an expensive luxury item – those who could afford them
probably could afford good meat).

Edelweiss is the national anthem of Austria (no … it was made famous by the 1959
musical *The Sound of Music* – the Austrian national anthem is *Land der Berge, Land
am Strome*).

And a few popular ones linked to learning

Listening to classical music enhances intelligence (based on a study from 1993 which
reported a short-term improvement in spatial reasoning). The effects of similar studies
do not support this.

Learners have a 'learning style' (e.g. visual, auditory or kinaesthetic) and learning
in this way will have a positive impact. The American Psychological Society (APA) has
carried out a number of studies to debunk this myth.

Certain physical exercises (e.g. Brain Gym) improve the ability to learn. This is generally considered 'pseudoscience' – peer-reviewed studies have not found any significant evidence to support this (Hyatt, 2007).

Figure 6.1   Common misconceptions

As you can see from the examples provided in Figure 6.1, most of the misconceptions have
a logical premise or are based on well-popularised ideas. Learning styles' theory is a typical example of this. When this idea was first introduced in the late 1980s, it gained a lot of
traction in education circles and was well promoted. It also has a logical basis – we have
many preferences in life, why not in the way we learn?

Assimilation and accommodation

Reducing the impact of well-embedded misconceptions is challenging – when we learn something new we make sense of it by relating it to what we already know. This is a notion that most teachers are familiar with and is a very traditional way of introducing a new topic; we might give a specific example from a previous lesson or put new information into an already-familiar context. When we *assimilate* we can take on new information without creating a new cognitive framework – the new is simply connected to the old. In contrast, when we have to *accommodate* knowledge this often means a revision of what we already 'know' and, as we generally have a tendency to hold on to our current knowledge, there will be an automatic barrier to this learning (Inhelder and Piaget, 1958). This is illustrated in simple terms in Figure 6.2. A child sees a four-legged creature but as the family pet is a dog, and also has four legs, she assimilates this information and calls the new animal a 'dog'. However, when she comes across another four-legged, of the feline variety, she notes it also has the same characteristics and calls this a dog. This misconception is corrected so she is able to assimilate the new information by making the connection to the other four-legged animal and noting some differences with the new one.

For young children, this adaptation is a more natural process, but young adults and mature learners are likely to have a tendency to overemphasise any information that supports current theories and discount, or even discredit, anything which challenges their current understanding. For this reason it is important that we create a positive and supportive learning environment so that new and old learning can be explored in a safe way. In addition, there are a number of strategies which help to accommodate new and sometimes challenging learning:

Addressing commonly-held misconceptions at the beginning of a unit prepares learners for the possibility that their current thinking may be challenged.

Cutting down on 'teacher talk' – we all know that lectures can be time efficient ways of getting across information, but we need to consider how we do this in a way that allows us to embed learning checks. Simple strategies for this include 'pause points' where we might take a break to check in with the group. In addition, lectures should be broken up by asking questions, and it is particularly useful to adopt a Socratic approach which allows you to probe thinking and challenge assumptions (the next section provides more information on this).

Using in-class activities which encourage learners to explore the lesson content also provide an opportunity to identify and correct any misconceptions.

Quizzing before and after a unit will help you to prepare for any misconceptions which already exist and follow up on any that may have developed.

Flipping the classroom – in this approach, learners are expected to access learning materials at home, for example, recordings, articles or reflections and then engage in problem-based learning activities when in the lesson. This strategy will prompt learners to clarify their understanding and provides the teacher with an opportunity to address any misconceptions which may arise.

Figure 6.2 Assimilation/accommodation

Getting active – most activity-based learning offers the opportunity to clarify understanding and can have a transformative effect on learning (but please take note of the 'learn from our mistakes' example). Using activities such as problem solving, and case studies can provide real life examples which encourage thinking about how topics are inter-related and encourage the transfer of learning.

There are numerous strategies which can be employed for this purpose and we have highlighted some of these in the 'Leveraging Learning Technology' section.

Leveraging learning technology

Assessment is quite simply where the use of ILT shines, particularly for formative assessment. There are a plethora of tools available to teachers for assessment at all levels, many of which provide instant feedback to learners and enhance engagement.

Some of the most common or most popular tools are quiz type tools that require learners to use their mobile phones to respond to questions that were pre-set/built by the teacher. Three of these, which also have banks of questions that teachers can modify or just use at will are Kahoot.it, Quizizz.com and Blooket.com. Socrative.com is similar to the other three; it is less game like but has some interesting features, like creating random teams (so learners aren't singled out) and an exit ticket (which asks learners to answer the question the teacher has written on the board and then what they have learned and need to work on more). Of the four of these, although they all have their uses, Quizizz.com is by far our favourite for a few reasons;

- It is very engaging and learners can even get power ups to boost their score.
- You can turn off timings so learners are less rushed, all of the questions appear on the learner's device and can be randomised so it doesn't matter if a learner shouts out.
- The report on the back end is excellent and will tell you how each learner did individually as well as the questions that the group as a whole best understood or struggled with the most.
- It has the broadest range of question types, meaning it is still usable for assessing slightly higher order thinking.
- There is a pay wall, but you can still do quite a lot on the free side of that wall.

There are also some great tools that allow you to design presentations with assessments built into them. Mentimeter.com allows you to design presentations and insert some useful activities like polls, questions and word walls. Nearpod.com is perhaps the best of these types of websites as it allows you to upload existing presentations (PowerPoints) and insert a range of interesting assessments between the slides. Nearpod assessments include activities such as, fill in the blank, a matching game, a drawing activity (which if you are creative can be really useful) and even game-style quizzes.

Many ILT tools have focused primarily on knowledge-level assessments for the simple reason that they are easier to do with automatic marking and feedback; the teacher simply tells the system the right answer. Higher-level thinking is much more difficult to assess in such a way and, as yet, teacher input is still required for feedback and development, this is an area where AI is likely to change have significant impact. That being said, there are some tools out there that do this well. Kialo.com (discussed in Chapter 3) is a debate tool which allows teachers to create a question, debate or argument, and learners can post arguments for and against with supporting evidence. Kialo is an excellent way to stimulate and facilitate discussion and even to get learners to plan their essays. Padlet.com is also an excellent tool for assessing at a higher level, as it can be used to allow learners to do research and post their findings, or to create a bank of evidence and resources as a whole class. Padlet is also an excellent tool for learners to create portfolios of evidence or to plan and track the progress of a project (perhaps posting weekly updates or reflections) and of course all Padlets can be shared with teachers to add comments and feedback.

If your learners do not have access to their own devices, then you may want to consider Plickers.com, which allows teachers to ask multiple choice or true/false questions and learners only need a printed QR code to respond. It is also worth noting that if you are in a school that uses Microsoft or Google, then their versions of forms allow you to create quizzes for learners. They may not be as game-like, but they can still be set to autocorrect, allow teachers to manually correct open questions and even email results to learners or parents.

There are many more assessment tools available to teachers and it is useful to add some variety to what you use. To help you with this it may be worth checking the full list of ILT tools outlined in the appendix and exploring the supporting Padlet page by scanning this QR code. Links to all of the tools discussed here can be found in the Chapter 6 section.

The importance of questioning

Checking on learning is an essential aspect of teaching. We need to be able to ascertain if learning has taken place, if further support is required or if an increased pace or level is needed. Questions help us to do this, but not all questions have equal impact; choosing the right type of question is very important and this can be challenging to do in a spontaneous way. Not surprisingly, teachers frequently check learning by using questions, yet according to Kerry (2002), 96 per cent of the questions we ask are 'lower order' questions. This means we might opt for questions which have right or wrong, yes or no answers, which often assess learning at a surface level. There is a reason these types of questions are popular. They are safe, they often confirm that we have taught something successfully and they don't interfere with the flow of the lesson. Often the surface knowledge answer we get gives us enough information to be able to move the lesson forwards but not the information that tells us deeper learning has taken place.

Introducing 'higher order' questioning helps us to judge how learners are using their learning, whether they can reflect on it, question and transfer it to a range of scenarios. This paves the way for deeper learning that goes beyond the superficial 'learning for the test' approach and equips our learners with skills that will be beneficial in all aspects of their lives. So, let's look at some of the types of questions and how you can employ them to the best effect.

Types of questions

There are many types of questions we can use including closed questions, which require short precise answers and check whether or not facts have been remembered, or open questions which can result in much deeper thinking; for example, 'Do you think education is a good thing?' (closed) or, 'why is education a good thing? (open). But if we want learners to develop their thinking a little further we might use a funnel approach and probing questions. Here we might ask something quite general, such as 'why is managing stress important?' and follow this by asking more specific questions, for example 'what techniques can be used to manage stress in the workplace? Why is that particular technique helpful?' By doing this we are encouraging learners to delve further into the topic, and we might also be probing to find out whether they are making assumptions. For example, 'What do we have to assume for this to be the case? Or what assumptions are we making?'

A useful strategy for probing learning is using the Socratic method. This is an effective tool for exploring thinking and encouraging reflection. The approach is based on six types of questions which have been outlined in Table 6.1.

Table 6.1 Examples of Socratic questions

Type of question	Example
Conceptual clarification – based on 'tell me more'. These questions prompt learners to make connections.	What exactly does this mean? How does this relate to what we have been talking about? Can you give me an example?
Probing assumptions – are questions used to challenge unquestioned assumptions or beliefs.	How did you choose those assumptions? What else could we assume?
Probing rationale – these questions are used to seek evidence for particular arguments.	How do you know this? What do you think causes ...? What evidence is there to support what you are saying?
Questioning viewpoints – these questions are used to explore perspectives.	What alternative ways could we look at this? What is the difference between ... and ...? What would [theorist] say about this?
Probing implications and consequences – these questions help to check if understanding and assumptions make sense.	What are the implications of ...? How does ... affect ...? How does ... fit with what we learnt before?
Questioning the question – this is simply a way of turning a question on itself so that learners see the value of exploring a topic through dialogue.	What was the point of asking that question? Why do you think I asked you this question?

How to use questions

Whilst choosing the type of question is important, the implementation is crucial for effective outcomes. We need to allow learners time to think through their responses and encourage them to acknowledge (and not be afraid of) any gaps in their learning. One strategy which is useful for this is the Pose, Pause, Pounce and Bounce model. The model is designed to give thinking time after posing the question before picking a learner to answer. Then, when an answer is received, it is bounced to someone else in order to elicit more detail. Here's how that might work in practice:

- Pose: 'Why is it important for children to learn to read?';
- Pause: wait at least ten seconds (it will seem like an age);
- Pounce: pick someone to answer the question;
- Bounce: bounce the question to another person by asking if they agree or have something to add.

The real value of this model lies with the bounce feature. When the first answer is given, it becomes the stepping stone to further information, building up the layers to higher order thinking. The strategy can also promote collaborative learning and increase learner confidence as they will soon learn that they don't have to get the right answer straight away. In fact, the strategy moves away from the 'only one right answer' approach which many learners can find intimidating. You may need to be prepared though. By anticipating responses, you can successfully direct the pounce and bounce element. Used consistently, learners become familiar with the format, and you may find that you have increased participation from the group.

One common issue with questioning is that teachers are uncomfortable when a question is met with no response. It is almost as if a great cavernous space has been created by the silence – even though the time between a question and response can be very small. There are two considerations here, teachers need to:

- Try to get comfortable with a short silence so that you leave sufficient time for learners to think of their answers.
- And … try not to answer the question for them!

Employing waiting time is essential, but it can be a balancing act. If too much time is given, interest may wane and if too little time is given learners may feel as if they have failed.

For many teachers a concern relating to questioning is that there are often one or two learners who provide most of the answers … so directing questions to individuals is important. In addition, it is important that the question and answer does not become a conversation between the teacher and the learner providing the response. To avoid this it is helpful to position yourself centrally so that you are interacting with the whole group.

Self and peer assessment

Earlier in the chapter we discussed the use of formative assessment in supporting learning. By embedding formative assessment within our teaching we are not only provided with feedback which helps teachers to adapt, we are also creating an environment which builds on learners' autonomy, self-esteem and motivation. Black and William's research (1998) starts from the premise that learning should be interactive, therefore learners must be actively involved in the assessment process. For this they need to:

* Understand their own role in relation to learning;
* Be able to understand and use feedback in a purposeful way;
* Be able to assess themselves.

In order to achieve this, teachers must give consideration to how assessment is organised and implemented within the classroom, in particular, the culture within which assessment activity takes place. Traditionally this would have been based on the idea that in order to be motivated, learners must be rewarded for their efforts so assessments would be linked to grades, class rankings and other extrinsic rewards. All well and good if you find assessment easy and sit comfortably within the 'top set'. But this focus does nothing to inspire those who do not do well in assessments, and, perhaps more surprisingly, does little to challenge high achievers! (Black and William, 1998).

When assessment becomes 'high stakes', it is likely that learners will concentrate their efforts on achieving the best marks, rather than focussing on improving their learning. This may lead to avoiding difficult tasks and limiting the development of higher-level thinking, as energy is likely to be expended on producing the right answers. In addition, learners who have not experienced success in previous assessments may be led to believe that they lack ability and therefore should not invest any effort in learning. In an ideal world, creating an environment in which grades were removed and feedback was seen as a reward in itself would be the best starting point – but most of us don't work within ideal frameworks. We need, therefore, to consider alternative ways of using assessment to enhance learning.

Self and peer assessment are fundamental strategies in encouraging learners to take responsibility for their own learning. Both provide the opportunity to critically evaluate performance as well as supporting the development of additional 'soft' skills such as collaboration and giving feedback to others. There are several benefits to using these approaches:

* Promotes self-reflection when considering own contribution to group projects;
* Encourages accountability for share of group workload;
* Develops understanding of learning objectives;
* Develops knowledge of own strengths and development areas;
* Can build confidence in working with others;
* Has the potential to foster respect and collaboration.

Reflection in self and peer assessment

Although there are many benefits to using both self and peer assessment activities, it is important to consider the potential drawbacks so that you can mitigate for these when creating the assessment opportunities:

* Some learners will struggle with assessing their peers and may give inappropriate or overly-positive feedback.

- Some learners may struggle to be constructive so there is a danger of giving overly critical feedback.
- There is the potential for 'hitchhiking' with some individuals not making a full contribution to a project.
- Assessments may not be taken as seriously as those carried out by the teacher.

Despite a few potential hurdles, the overarching benefit of using self and peer assessment is that it gives learners far more autonomy and in turn encourages them to take responsibility for their learning, both essential steppingstones in becoming 'expert learners'. Reflection is a key part of this process and by using reflective thinking to evaluate learning, it is possible to highlight specific strategies which have been effective, as well as those that were less effective, enabling learners to transfer skills and knowledge gained in one activity, to future assignments. Ertmer and Newby's work evidences the success of this approach, suggesting that the 'expert learner' is one who can reflect on their own performance, and then deliberately seek the strategies needed to achieve their desired learning goals (Ertmer and Newby, 1996).

Encouraging learner reflection

What strategies could you use to encourage learners to reflect on their learning and consider how they might transfer what they have learnt to different situations?

Teacher feedback

Throughout this chapter we have discussed how assessment can be used to improve learning in two fundamental ways:

- Providing teachers with information which allows them to adapt their teaching;
- Providing learners with information which allows them to adapt their approaches to learning.

It is most certainly a two-way process. Assessment by its very nature is an interaction between a range of elements. We could view it as a multi-faceted conversation between teacher, learner, feedback from and feedback to learners. Each of these individual facets providing information for progression.

The feedback we provide to learners is an essential function of the teaching role, yet so often is one that seems to fall short when it comes to its effectiveness. It is not unusual for learners to complain that they don't understand the feedback they have been given, or to say that they are not sure how they could improve their work in the future. Very often these grievances are justified. So, given that this is such an important part of the teacher's role, why aren't we better at it? There probably isn't a single answer to that question – we might need to consider culture, subject requirements, school and college policy to name but a few. However, often, the issue lies with where feedback is focussed. If there is a focus on

Table 6.2 Judgemental and constructive feedback

Judgemental feedback	Constructive feedback
Makes comparisons with others/grading.	Is based on clear criteria and provides information about the extent to which these have been met/ not met.
Has a focus on the grade or what is needed to pass, generating the 'right answer syndrome'.	Has a focus on information about improvements and effective learning techniques.
Generates a sense of blaming (mistakes are shameful).	Generates a blame-free approach (mistakes are opportunities to learn).
Learning is seen as a judgement (am I good/ not good at this?).	Learning is seen as an end in itself (I may not have done this perfectly but I have learnt something useful).

the giving of grades, and 'justifying' grade decisions, rather than on how future perform-ance might be improved, it is likely that the feedback simply becomes a statement of the obvious. For example: 'You provided an adequate introduction to the topic and included all of the key points. You discussed ... then added some detail about ... finally, you provided a good conclusion.'

The feedback might be enhanced by adding words like 'good' or 'excellent' at various points, but what does that tell the learner about the specifics of their work? How does the learner know what an adequate, as opposed to good introduction is? Similarly, what specifically was good about the conclusion and how might they repeat that in future assessments?

Feedback has a powerful influence on learning but for it to be effective it needs to be accompanied by 'feedforward'. It is also important that feedback takes a constructive, rather than judgemental approach, as outlined in Table 6.2.

It seems like a simple thing to provide good quality, informative feedback doesn't it? But don't be fooled. There is an art to this and one which may initially be supported by the use of a model. In general, feedback is more effective when it provides clear guidance and is focussed on specific goals. One way of structuring this is to answer three questions:

- Where am I going?
- How am I going?
- Where to next?

(Hattie and Timperley, 2007)

This provides a structure to close the gap between current understanding or performance and the desired end point. In addition, the use of questions emphasises the learner's role in the process. Whilst the teacher can provide clear feedback on current performance and guidance on steps forward, it is the learner's responsibility to increase efforts by employing effective strategies. As outlined in Figure 6.3, it is also important to address each of the questions at four levels; task, process, self-regulation and self.

By answering the four questions suggested in this model it is possible to provide personalised feedback to each learner and to address key aspects of a given assessment.

Effective Feedback

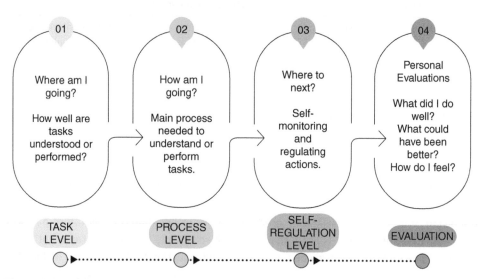

Figure 6.3 Feedback model
Source: Adapted from Hattie and Timperley, 2007

Task level feedback will focus on the learning intent and any specific requirements of a task, whereas process level feedback will be aimed at the skills and strategies required to complete the task. Self-regulatory feedback requires the learner to evaluate their own performance (based on your comments) and use relational thinking to make comparisons with assessment criteria or intended learning. Finally, evaluation provides the opportunity for the learner to highlight what they have learnt and can transfer to other situations. As these final sections are situated with the learner it is recommended that feedback also includes a verbal element so that teacher and learner can discuss next steps.

Enhancing learner reflection

What strategies could you employ to encourage learners to use feedback to improve their future performance?

Learn from our experience

Throughout this chapter we have promoted the importance of embedding formative feedback opportunities to enhance learning. It is fair to say we might even have presented this as something of a panacea for the perfect learning environment. But of course, perfection isn't usually that easy and sometimes we can overplay a particular strategy. This anecdote is taken from the experience of one of the authors so is written as a personal reflection.

> I was quite excited to carry out this observation. It was with a beauty therapy teacher who had really engaged with the course and continually tried to adapt her teaching based on her own learning. She was the perfect student! Even more interesting for me was that this was a theory lesson, so it was much more challenging to motivate the learners (who very often want to focus on perfecting their craft). It started well with an engaging online quiz. This was focussed on the previous week's lesson and used a piece of software the teacher had been introduced to quite recently. The learners were very engaged, almost battling to answer the questions first. A very positive start! Next came another online activity ... different software, taking the questions one step further. Still, the learners remained engaged. This was followed by another formative assessment activity ... and another ... And yet another.

It was clear within this particular observation that the student had taken on board the importance of formative assessment. What she had forgotten was the need for some instruction. As we stated at the very beginning of this chapter, 'there is no teaching without assessment'. We stand by that statement but are reminded that assessment, whilst a foundation of great teaching, is simply a part of the process. Great teaching also requires some teaching!

Summary

In this chapter we have focussed on the importance of formative assessment in relation to improving teaching and enhancing learning. We have explored how assessment can be used to address misconceptions and close gaps in learning, as well as strategies which will help to create 'expert' learners.

References

Black, P. and William, D. (1998) 'Assessment and Classroom Learning', *Assessment in Education*, 5: 7–74. doi: 10.1080/0969595980050102

Ertmer, P.A. and Newby, P. J. (1996) 'The Expert Learner: Strategic, Self-Regulated and Reflective', *Instructional Science*, (24):1–24.

Festinger, L. (1957) *A Theory of Cognitive Dissonance*. Stanford, CA: Stanford University Press.

Freire, P. (1998) *Pedagogy of Freedom: Ethics, Democracy and Civic Courage*. Washington, DC: Lanham, Rowman & Littlefield Publishers.

Hattie, J. and Timperley, H. (2007) 'The Power of Feedback', *Review of Educational Research*, 1(77): 81–112. doi: 10.3102/003465430298487.

Hyatt, K. J. (1 April, 2007) 'Brain Gym®: Building Stronger Brains or Wishful Thinking?', *Remedial and Special Education*, 28(2): 117–124. doi:10.1177/07419325070280020201. S2CID 145748559.

Inhelder, B. and Piaget, J. (1958) *The Growth of Logical Thinking from Childhood to Adolescence*. New York: Basic Books.

Kerry, T. (2002) *Mastering Teaching Skills: Explaining and Questioning*. Oxford: OUP.

Savion, L. (2009) 'Clinging to Discredited Beliefs: The Larger Cognitive Story', *Journal of the Scholarship of Teaching and Learning*, (9): 81–92.

Speckesser, S., Runge, J., Foliono, F., Bursnall, M., Hudson-Sharp, N., Rolfe, H. and Anders, J. (2018) *Embedding Formative Assessment, Evaluation Report and Executive Summary*. Millbank: Education Endowment Foundation.

7 Challenging thinking

Introduction

One of the most difficult tasks that any teacher faces is encouraging their students to become independent; to be able to go that bit further. Independent learners are those who can use the information the teacher provides to best effect. They interact with it, question it, transfer it to different scenarios and ultimately develop their own ideas about the subject. If we were to suggest a model of the perfect learner, this would be it ... curious, 'bright', self-motivated and showing a genuine interest in the subject being taught. But why does it seem there are fewer learners in our classes who match this description? This may simply be a perception, but it does make us wonder whether there is something that we can do as teachers to help our learners progress from being satisfied with simply getting a good grade, to those who seek out opportunities to develop their learning? In other words, can we help our students to become 'expert learners'?

The objective of this chapter is to provide some ideas for helping learners to become 'expert learners', the learners that Ertmer and Newby (1996) describe as strategic, self-regulated and reflective. Learners who are able to set their own goals, and continuously use reflection to evaluate their progress (Zimmerman, 2002). As teachers we recognise that all our students have different needs, wants, motivations etc.; some may not be able to achieve the status of being an 'expert learner' and others may need a lot of help along the way. Nevertheless, by incorporating various 'teaching tactics' into our plans for teaching it is possible that *all* our students will absorb at least some of the skills and strategies of the expert learner subliminally, lodging them in their long-term memory where they will be able (perhaps unwittingly!) to call upon them to transfer prior learning of one sort or another from one context to another in later life.

Memory and learning

Before we can help our learners to become expert learners we need to have some understanding of how students learn and how they store things in their memories. Willingham (2002:6) suggests that the 'human mind appears to be biased towards learning the surface features of problems ... [rather than] ... the deep structure' of knowledge. In other words, students are likely to accept and memorise processes and facts (the surface

DOI: 10.4324/9781003385905-8

features) when presented to them without fully understanding them, in preference to thinking about them and interacting with the information to establish the underlying principles or ideas (the deeper structures). The problem with surface learning is that it is exactly that – something that is not connected with other learning so that it remains an isolated piece of knowledge or a fact situated in the context in which it was learned. This lack of integration with other learning means that it is somewhat inflexible, and its usefulness is limited. However, it can become useful or flexible if it can be 'accessed out of the context in which it was learned and applied to new contexts' (Willingham 2002:5). For example, learning how to calculate how much liquid a cylinder can hold may be something that is in the school curriculum, but to most people it's just a piece of isolated knowledge until they have to work out the most cost-effective way of buying the tins of fizzy pop they need to buy for thirsty children.

As you will remember from reading Chapter 3, the memory is divided into three areas, short-term, long-term and working memory, each with their own specialist function. All new knowledge and learning are initially received as surface learning and placed by the brain into the short-term working memory, which can hold only a limited amount of information. From there it can be passed into the long-term memory, which has a pretty unlimited capacity, and either incorporated into existing schema or branched off to form a new schema (Sweller et al., 2016). Again, this is something that was covered in Chapter 3 so if you would like a more detailed reminder it might be worth referring back to that chapter. With the development of large numbers of increasingly complex and sophisticated schema in the long-term memory, connections between different elements evolve, and the level of understanding increases.

One of the first things we want to know before we begin to teach is what the students already know or can remember. This is often done through some sort of re-cap of previous learning, perhaps by asking questions to ascertain the students' recollection of what was taught in a previous lesson or lessons, or to help you to establish their familiarity with a new subject. Questions might be posed to test mechanistic or surface learning through recalling of facts or information previously imparted. Alternatively, more complicated questions, often posed in the form of problems, which require students to *use* existing knowledge, can be employed. The second type of question must go beyond simple recall in order to test deeper learning. For example – remember Iniko, the puppy you met in Chapter 5? He recently went to the vets for a check-up after some medical problems. Whilst he was waiting for the practitioner in the reception area, a group of students studying veterinary medicine arrived to start the practical phase of their studies. The vet came into reception and put Iniko (who they had never seen before) on the floor where the students could see him before starting to ask them questions about him. Initially he asked them what they could tell about him by looking at him (and in his case listening to him as he was protesting loudly at this point!); this was followed up by asking them to draw on their previous learning to determine if there was anything physically wrong with him. By asking them to utilise their deeper learning in a practical context not only was he testing their recall skills but also checking their understanding.

Most of us will have asked questions about prior learning to check student knowledge and/or prior learning at the start of the lesson, and been faced with blank expressions on learners' faces, particularly when posing questions designed to probe deep learning. At this point many teachers would simply revert to asking questions which rely on recall (surface learning) rather than understanding (deeper learning) to reassure ourselves that the students have 'learned' something from preceding lessons.

As the examples in this chapter suggest, if we want to help our learners develop into expert learners, there are two issues we need to consider:

- How can teachers help students move information from their short-term memory into their long-term memories?
- How can teachers help students develop the skill of deep learning?

The influence of others on learning

Having a basic understanding of how the memory processes and stores information is useful, but there is more to learning than just processing information. New-born children only experience sensory learning gained through touch, taste, hearing, sight or smell which gives initial information to the brain which at this stage is effectively a *tabula rasa*. As the child develops, language becomes an increasingly key factor in the learning process. It allows them to interact with others and by so doing facilitates their understanding of social situations by enabling them to interpret the context and the actions of others.

Vygotsky (1978), however, argued that theorists such as Piaget placed insufficient emphasis on the role of language in learning, and by concentrating on the influence of external stimuli he also overlooked the importance the cultural aspect. Although individuals are the sum of their unique experiences, for Vygotsky, language and culture are shared social phenomena which form the framework through which the individual learns to interpret and develop meaning of the world. The experience of sharing language and culture initially facilitates an interpsychological level of learning, i.e. the sharing of information between individuals or groups. A second or higher level of learning, the intrapsychological level occurs individually when first level learning is challenged in some way. This challenge (which can be created by others or the context itself) causes the individual both to reflect on, and interact with, the initial learning stimulating the process of deeper learning. Knowledge and understanding for Vygotsky are not something which are simply constructed by the individual but are co-constructed through interaction with others. We can take from this idea that for students to develop new knowledge and understanding the process of learning needs to be a shared rather than individual process. One which is the result of social contact, cultural interaction and shared language with the process of learning itself being as important as the acquisition of the new knowledge.

Any language is simply a code for expressing thoughts, emotions and of course shared experiences, that includes learning which can be understood by other people. If you work with young people you may well have found that at times they use language in a way which is unfamiliar to you. We have all been confused by students describing something as 'sick', which we took to mean something was bad, when in fact it was the opposite. By adapting language in this way they were developing a code through which they could express themselves to those within their peer group but which excluded those not included in the group (such as teachers and parents) – that is, until the code was cracked! When teaching we need to include all our students in the learning process and one of the ways of doing this is to ensure that they all learn and use the terms associated with the specific subject. By doing this they are becoming part of an exclusive club of sorts – one with shared language and terms which others who are not studying the same subject are not familiar with – sharing the 'secret language' of the subject as part of a 'club' boosts learners' self-confidence, fosters their sense of belonging and helps develop a group identity.

Thinking about language

Think about the subject that you teach and identify some of the specific terms that you use. How do you pass on those terms to your learners? How do you introduce them to new terms? How do you ensure that they understand them? How do you model their use?

Scaffolding

The importance of language in learning was also recognised by Bruner (1978) who saw its critical role in students being able to understand and develop concepts and ideas. Bruner also recognised that this development needed to be supported by others within the learning environment, a process described as scaffolding. For Bruner (1978), scaffolding is a structured interaction between an adult and a student whereby the teacher guides the student towards the achievement of a specific goal by 'reduc[ing] the degrees of freedom in carrying out [a] task so that the [student] can concentrate on the difficult task they are undertaking' (Bruner, 1978:19).

Limiting choice in this way might initially seem to be counterintuitive if we are asking students to research or explore a subject. By limiting the students' freedom to seek their own solutions, he argues that students can be guided by reducing the 'trial and error' aspect of learning, a process which can lead many students to stray from the task in hand (or 'disappear down rabbit holes' as a colleague describes it) leading to frustration and misunderstanding (Figure 7.1). A colleague uses this approach very successfully with his learners – he offers them a choice between three or four different options (all of which he knows will lead to the same goal but offer different ways of achieving it). The students feel that they have options and autonomy in their learning as they can make a choice, and he knows that by limiting their choice they will arrive successfully at the end objective without wasting time and energy – a win-win strategy!

Learning can also be successfully scaffolded by breaking the task into bite size pieces (a process commonly described as chunking the information or process, which we covered in Chapter 3). This approach makes the task seem less daunting and can act as a motivational tool as students can not only see a way forward, but they can also see what they have achieved. Whatever format scaffolding takes, the actions of the teacher in the process are critical. All interaction with the learners during this process provides teachers

Figure 7.1 Down the rabbit hole

with the opportunity to highlight important areas, model good practice and correct any misconceptions. The learner can then imitate what the teacher is demonstrating and apply this to the task they are completing.

Although the teacher is important in helping students develop new knowledge there are other elements, such peer interaction, which can be just as important. Collaboration with peers could help individuals move from their actual level of development (what they already 'know') to their potential level of development. A range of exchanges between learners can be used here, for example group discussions which require learners to defend, justify, clarify and communicate their ideas with others in a temporary 'community of practice' (Lave and Wenger, 2003). If their ideas are accepted, then they become shared knowledge through which the individual is able to access a deeper level of learning. As we discussed in Chapter 5, learning through collaborative or co-operative group activities is one of the strategies that can be implemented in planning lessons to promote deeper learning but we do need to remember that, as noted by Burke (2011), not everyone responds well to this approach, so as with any strategy, we cannot become over-reliant on it.

Checking the level of learning

Think about a recent lesson and any questions you may have used to start the lesson. Write down the questions you can remember. Then, analyse the words and the question structure and consider these in relation to level of challenge. Were there any questions which were simply a recall of information? If so, how could you adapt these so that they are checking deep learning?

If you were aiming to check deep learning through questioning and found that the level of understanding was not quite as deep as you wished, then your next step is likely to be going over the elements students are struggling with. Simply repeating the information might help with recall skills, but it will be a 'turn-off' for students who have heard it all before and didn't understand it the first-time round. You may well need to consider a different approach to try to grab their attention and to get them to think about the underlying principles which will promote deep learning. One way of doing this is through dialogic teaching, which will help you establish more precisely where students are having difficulty and challenge them by asking them to reflect on and analyse learning.

Dialogic teaching and learning

Successful teaching and learning depend on 'the extent to which instruction requires students to think, not just to report someone else's thinking' (Nystrand et al., 1997, 72). This often means that we are not accepting first responses unless they happen to be extremely well thought out. In the general scheme of things it means we will use questions which probe the answers in order to challenge and extend thinking. This type of challenge might sound harsh … but of course it doesn't have to be confrontational and to get things started you can use some of the Socratic questions outlined in Chapter 6. An effective method of challenge is the use of dialogic teaching (Alexander, 2020). When we use this approach, we are encouraging discussion but one in which the student 'voice' is as important as that of the teacher. It is in essence a professional discussion. As a method to facilitate deep learning it has sound philosophical roots being based on the Socratic practice of disciplined, thoughtful dialogue. In this approach questioning is used to encourage students to examine ideas in depth and ascertain their validity for themselves rather than simply echoing the thoughts of the teacher and not only do learners have the opportunity to challenge their own thinking, they will also be developing their use of language, which as Halliday suggests is the foundation of learning (1993).

Dialogic teaching, rather than using questioning to simply assess knowledge,

uses questioning as a means of involving students in the learning process, encouraging them to take some ownership of the subject under discussion by sharing information and opinions whilst simultaneously extending and deepening their knowledge and refining their thinking skills.

There are five main principles which need to be employed in dialogic teaching and learning. To be effective it needs students to be:

Collective – working together in groups to tackle a learning task.

Reciprocal – participating in the group by listening to each other, sharing their ideas and considering and respecting the views and opinions put forward by others.

Supportive – able to bring their ideas, theories and comments to the table without fear of being judged and through discussion they are able to mediate their views and reach a collective understanding of the subject or theory under discussion.

Cumulative – to develop their own contributions and build on the thoughts and opinions of those of others to form a logical sequence of ideas and understanding.

Purposeful – to take part in planned discussions. Although open and non-judgmental in form these need to be structured by the teacher to move student learning towards a specific objective or learning aim (Main, n.d.).

As a teaching strategy the dialogic method can be planned into lessons in a number of formats. For example, it can be used in whole class teaching where all learners can be involved in a single learning task, in teacher-led group work, in learner-led group work or in a one-to-one discussion. However, a note of warning; as with any form of group activity, before embarking on this type of approach it may be advisable to negotiate, confirm, periodically review and possibly reinforce some ground rules with students to ensure that they adhere to the principles outlined above. During the dialogic process, discussions entail an open exchange of (sometimes challenging) views or explore issues, ideas and problems, and care should be taken by the teacher to ensure that the British Values which will be outlined in Chapter 8, are observed. The discussions themselves can be teacher, student or group led, but it may be necessary for the teacher to scaffold the dialogue by encouraging students to approach the subject in diverse ways, for example by:

- Asking and encouraging questions which require more than just recall;
- Following up on answers or views and building on these rather than just acknowledging them;
- Encouraging feedback which not only recognises the response but informs and promotes forward (or further and deeper) thinking on the part of participants (Rich et al, 2017);
- Encouraging contributions from others which are extended rather than fragmented so that exchanges form links in a chain to create more coherent and deepening lines of enquiry.

Using dialogic teaching

Take a look at one of your recent lesson plans or think about a recent lesson and the sort of activities you included. Was there an opportunity for you to use dialogic teaching to engage your students in the learning process? How do you think they would respond to this method of learning?

By acquiring personal knowledge and experience of learning processes students begin to develop the ability for the individual to transfer their existing knowledge and skills to new situations, something which is a primary objective of education as it enables students to utilise their learning in real life and post-education contexts.

Transfer of learning

Earlier in the chapter Willingham's notions of flexible and inflexible learning were introduced – surface learning being narrow and inflexible and deep learning providing flexibility which can be applied in a different context. Many learners are adept at surface learning and if they are particularly interested in the subject, possibly some elements of deeper learning. However, knowledge can become siloed – we learn things in a given context and find it difficult to transfer it elsewhere. This might be because human memory tends to be context dependent; new information is 'tied' to the situation in which it is experienced, making it difficult to apply in alternative situations. Have you ever had the experience whereby you know you have taught something really well, you have checked learning frequently and learners always give expected answers (i.e. ones which suggest they understand?). Perhaps you are asking them to follow a process or apply some key principles in a given scenario? In class they get it right every time. Then the exam comes around and the paper is expecting them to do exactly the thing you have taught them (and the thing they have demonstrated so well in practice exercises) but, the paper uses a different context, it sets a different type of scene and maybe uses different language. What happens? Do your learners immediately work out that what they are being asked to do is exactly the same thing that they have done lots of times before ... or do they panic, thinking that the different context is in fact asking for something completely different to what they had learnt?

This is a significant barrier which is made more significant when learners only have a limited understanding of what they have learnt. Such difficulties are likely to cause problems when they come across different language or are expected to use their learning in a different way. However, when learners develop their understanding to incorporate breadth and depth, transfer of learning to an alternative context becomes much easier. Learning transfer can take two forms, near transfer and far transfer (Barnett and Ceci, 2002):

- Near transfer occurs when there is an overlap between the context and conditions of the original learning and the new situation. For example, we might learn essay writing skills in an English class and can use this to write an assignment in history. Here the conditions are very similar, and we are simply making a slight change to the context.
- Far transfer occurs when the new situation is very different from that in which the learning took place. For example, we may have learnt basic statistics in economics and can transfer this to another subject where we have to analyse some data.

Helping learners to develop the skills necessary to transfer learning from one context to another can be tricky. Bjork and Bjork (2011) suggest that 'desirable difficulties' that can be planned into lessons by the teacher as part of the overall teaching programme may be one way to enhance learners' abilities in this area. In a sense, what we are doing here is 'shaking up' the learning environment by posing challenges which on the surface seem to slow down the initial rate of learning but which over time, actually enhance it. Think about what happens when we change the structure of a class, perhaps when we start with something different which is a step away from the normal routine. Do you remember the 'learn from our experience' story in Chapter 2 when we described the lesson with no objectives? This situation created a lot of discomfort for the learners because it was quite different to what they were used to, but whilst the initial discomfort was evident, the overall learning (and certainly the retention of information) was higher than usual. So, rather than relying on a narrow range of teaching methods (and we all have one or two that we tend to favour and use regularly), it is suggested that we vary teaching approaches and learning activities. In addition, introducing a range of revision or practice tasks spaced out at regular intervals in the teaching schedule, provides opportunities for learners to recall information and adapt it to a range of scenarios. If learning is revisited regularly and complexity is gradually increased, this provides learners with the opportunity to build on their learning and reflect on any potential gaps in knowledge. Interweaving other tasks, topics or subjects, so that learners revisit previously taught information several times over a period of time, also generates deeper understanding of the subject, which in turn supports the ability to transfer this to other situations. Teachers can further support this by modelling the ways in which aspects of learning can be transferred from one situation to another.

Strategies for enhancing learning transfer

There are five simple approaches which can support learners in developing the skills to transfer learning:

1. *Explicit teaching* – obvious as this seems, sometimes we need to point out where learning may be useful. This means discussing where current learning can be applied in other parts of life. For example if we learnt the skill of developing a balanced argument in order to complete an essay, we might be able to transfer this to the workplace when we are convincing our boss we need a pay rise.
2. *Learning in groups* – provides the opportunity to collaborate and build skills that will be welcome in the workplace.
3. *Use metaphor or analogies* – by comparing one thing that is familiar with something else we are modelling learning transfer. For example, we might suggest that a heart might work like a pump, or a well-known story might give us some insight. Just think about Peter Pan, the boy who never grew up ... a story which focussed on the importance of imagination, positive thought, bravery and kinship.
4. *Reflection* – encourage your learners to reflect on their own learning and on the strategies that work best for them. For example, if planning an outline of an assignment helped them to organise their work in one subject, could this be transferred to another?
5. *Generalisation* – by asking learners to generalise broader principles from specific situations we can create a framework for further learning.

Learn from our experience

This is a reflection from one of the authors, so is written in first person.

I was once assigned to teach a unit on the physics of car traffic accidents. Even though I have taught some maths, my degree is in Social Sciences, so this was somewhat of a learning curve for me. Whilst teaching the unit I had to ensure that learners were able to understand and calculate SUVAT equations (equations of motion). I spent an entire lesson explaining the meaning of each variable and walking learners through each of the five equations and giving them practice examples to calculate. At the end of the lesson, I asked a series of questions to assess their understanding of what we had been doing for the last one and a half hours and it quickly became clear they had no idea of the point of the lesson, or where they would need these equations. They had seemed to be engaged for an entire lesson, they had completed the activities, but had not fully understood any of it!

Reflecting on this event, I realised I had to take a different approach and would need to completely reteach the lesson. The next week, I began the lesson by calling a 'mulligan', I asked the group to pretend the previous lesson had never happened. I was honest and told them I had taken the wrong approach and that it wasn't their fault that they didn't understand SUVAT equations, it was mine. This time we watched videos of crash tests and after each one we looked at the variables of the vehicle in the videos and made predictions of the damage after choosing and calculating the appropriate equation. We had all left the previous lesson frustrated because we felt we hadn't achieved anything, but the energy in this lesson was completely different. Using real-life examples helped learners visualise the variables in question – we went beyond words on a page.

Although we were still discussing physics, learners were transferring what had been, until that time, abstract knowledge to live examples in an attempt explain the outcomes. Obviously, most teachers won't have to call a mulligan on an entire lesson, but in doing so, it was possible to earn the trust and respect of the learners. Modelling, in this case showing examples of the theory in practice, is undoubtedly at its most effective if learners can relate to the model in some way. It may be necessary to use more than one model or example to show how concepts can be applied in different contexts.

Activity

Reflect on a recent lesson. How did you model the transfer of knowledge/learning? Did you include any models to demonstrate theory in practice? What was the reaction of the students? Do you feel that you used the right model or is there something else that you could have included which might have been more helpful?

Figure 7.2 Kialo

Leveraging learning technology

One particularly effective method of driving deep learning is the 'big question'. In line with the notion of Socratic questioning mentioned earlier in this chapter, the 'big question' is simply an open-ended question that does not have a clear right or wrong answer but facilitates debate. Although most online tools are geared toward assessing surface learning, there are a few that can drive deeper learning by getting learners to apply knowledge to a variety of contexts or pursue 'big questions'.

Kialo (referenced in Chapters 3 and 6) is one of the best tools out there for this. Kialo is a debate platform that allows teachers to post a question and invite learners to respond for or against. One of the best features of the tool is that it allows for sub-debates to develop as learners can refute or support individual points and as the debate develops the site creates a mind map (like the image in Figure 7.2).

Learners can also support their arguments by adding links to sources, supporting websites and even videos, and teachers can set tasks that require learners to include these. As an alternative, teachers could also use Padlet which works well when using shelf mode to create columns for multiple arguments around a question and assigning learners or groups to defend those arguments with points and supporting evidence.

Digital storytelling is a really useful and creative strategy whereby learners use digital tools to create a narrative. This could be as simple as using a collection of images and overlaying text, or combining video clips with narration in more of a documentary style. It sounds complicated but if you use the right tools it isn't and given the potential impact it is worth spending a little time developing this skillset. Storytelling is a very effective method of learning as it drives students to combine surface knowledge with their imaginations and apply this to real world contexts.

There are a number of video editing tools that were explored in Chapter 4. iMovie for Apple devices, Windows Video Editor for PCs or Moovly.com are great online tools for this. There are a multitude of video editing tools available for students and teachers to use and most are pretty similar overall in terms of their capability; it is more about which ones you have easy access to.

Remember that all of the tools discussed here, as well as some examples of digital stories can be found on the companion Padlet page, which is accessed by scanning the QR code.

Summary

In this chapter we have looked at how challenging students' thinking can develop their skills as learners. Not all our students can become expert learners, but many of them will with your help and support. Understanding how the memory works with information to develop deep learning as opposed to surface learning was our first port of call. We have looked at the part you play in influencing students' development by introducing activities which actively involve students in the learning process. In this context we looked at different dialogic strategies and using modelling as ways to encourage students to transfer learning from one situation to another.

References

Alexander, R. (2020) *A Dialogic Teaching Companion*. Abingdon: Routledge.

Barnett, S. M. and Ceci, S. U. (2002) 'When and Where Do We Apply What We Learn? A Taxonomy for Far Transfer', *Psychological Bulletin*, 128: 612–637. doi: https://doi.org/10.1037//0033-2909.128.4.612.

Bjork, E. L. and Bjork, R. A. (2011) 'Making Things Hard on Yourself, but in a Good Way: Creating Desirable Difficulties to Enhance Learning', in M. A Gernsbacher, R. W. Pew, L. M. Hough and J. R. Pomerantz (eds), *Psychology and the Real World: Essays Illustrating Fundamental Contributions to Society*. New York: Worth Publishers, pp. 56–64.

Bruner, J. S. (1978) 'The Role of Dialogue in Language Acquisition', in A. Sinclair, R., J. Jarvelle and W. J. M. Levelt (eds), *The Child's Concept of Language*. New York: Springer-Verlag, pp. 241–256.

Burke, A. (2011) 'Group Work: How to Use Groups Effectively', *The Journal of Effective Teaching*, 11(2): 87–95.

Ertmer, P. A. and Newby, T. J. (1996) 'The Expert Learner: Strategic, Self-Regulated, and Reflective', *Instructional Science*, 24: 1–24.

Halliday, M. A. K. (1993) 'Towards a language-Based Theory of Learning', *Linguistics in Education*, 5(2): 93–116.

Lave, J. and Wenger, E. (2003) *Situated Learning: Legitimate Peripheral Participation*. Cambridge: Cambridge University Press Cambridge

Main, P. (n.d.) *Dialogic Teaching: A classroom Guide for Better Thinking and Talking*. Available at www.structural-learning.com/post/how-to-use-dialogic-pedagogy-the-key-to-powerful-teaching [Accessed 10 April 2023].

Nystrand, M., Wu, L.L., Gamoran, A., Zeiser, S. and Long, D.A. (1997) 'Questions in Time: Investigating the Structure and Dynamics of Unfolding Classroom Discourse', *Discourse Processes*, 35 (2): 135–198.

Rich, P. R., Van Loon, M. H., Dunlosky, J., and Zaragoza, M. S. (2017) 'Belief in Corrective Feedback for Common Misconceptions: Implications for Knowledge Revision', *Journal of Experimental Psychology: Learning, Memory, and Cognition*, 43(3): 492–501.

Sweller, J. (2016) 'Working Memory, Long-term Memory and Instructional Design', *Journal of Applied Research in Memory and Cognition*, 5: 360–367.

Vygotsky, L. S. (1978) *Mind in Society: The Development of Higher Psychological Processes*. Cambridge, MA: Harvard University Press.

Willingham, D. T. (2002) Ask the Cognitive Scientist. Inflexible Knowledge: The First Step to Expertise. www.researchgate.net/publication/234665275_.

Zimmerman, B. J. (2002) 'Becoming a Self-Regulated Learner: An Overview', *Theory Into Practice*, 41(2): 64–67.

8 Embedding the 'added extras'

Introduction

Plato saw education as a form of social justice and as a way of eradicating evil, believing that if all citizens were educated and all had an understanding of 'good', the wellbeing of humankind would be enhanced and society would become self-regulating. Therefore a 'just' society would be one that tried to give the best education to all of its citizens, in accordance with their ability. He also had some very definite views about what should be taught and when, believing that stages of learning ranged from basic to advanced and technical. This is not dissimilar to the ways in which modern education systems are organised. In order to maintain this utopian society, Plato stated that it was the government's (or ruler's) responsibility to maintain control over the education system, regulating what the people were taught. This was seen as a way of shaping people's beliefs and instilling a desire to undertake their roles in society with a sense of devotion. Again, the similarities are evident. Education is about much more than knowing or being able to do something. Compulsory schooling has a role in ensuring that everyone has the knowledge which allows them to function in society – reading, writing and numeracy being some of the more obvious contenders here. But what of the other things we need to learn? The content related to core subjects, the skills we need for personal and professional development? Developing the ability to cope with everyday pressures? The list is potentially endless and often these things are seen as 'extras' which are over and above the teaching of subject content. We might call them the 'hidden curriculum' even when they are actually quite overt!

Although few would argue that learners need the opportunity to develop skills beyond those related to a subject, there can be resistance from learners – and teachers. Learners may not see immediate relevance and perhaps feel that some of the 'soft' skills, such as working with others and respecting diversity, are not as important as learning about a subject. As for teachers, there is another dilemma – teachers are well aware that most curricula are packed with content, and they are also aware that there is very little time to cover everything as thoroughly as they would like. It's quite a challenge to include everything without tying yourself in knots. In this chapter we will endeavour to consider how core subjects can be refocused to help learners see that this all-important additional learning can be seamlessly interwoven into the current curriculum.

DOI: 10.4324/9781003385905-9

What are added extras?

There are many views on the purpose of education and how this influences what should be taught, especially in schools. After all, compulsory education is something that the vast majority of people have experienced. Schools have a captive audience, and this is the only place where we can guarantee that learners should be in regular daily attendance for at least nine months of the year. If those in power want to influence our society, this is the very place to do it. The downside to this is the very real phenomena of 'curriculum dumping' – if there is something in society that should be fixed, add it to the list of things schools should teach. Indeed, a study of what schools should teach identified 213 items to be added to the main curriculum (Burke and Lehain, 2018), including enterprise, first aid, internet safety, resilience – the biggest three categories accounted for 114 of these and included:

> Health (68 proposals)
> Finance (24 proposals)
> Technology (22 proposals)
>
> (Burke and Lehain, 2018:3)

Whilst schools often bear the brunt of this type of initiative, other phases of education have not been let off the hook. In further education, the implementation of 'extras' such as numeracy, literacy and digital skills was (and remains) the subject of much discussion and has resulted in government reports such as the Dearing Review (1997) and the Tomlinson Report (2004). These reports recognised the importance of practical skills both to the individual and the economy and deemed the acquisition of these skills to be something educators in Further Education should include within the teaching of vocational subjects. With the passage of time, society has changed and other priorities have evolved, for example British values, employability skills, behaviour management, communication skills, mental health, wellbeing and sustainability.

High expectations of the education sector have led to it being seen as something of a panacea for society's ailments. Schools, colleges and universities do have a significant support role to play here, but they can't and perhaps shouldn't attempt to do everything. That said, as teachers we all recognise that our influence extends beyond the classroom and that education can be:

- A vehicle for social change;
- A support to economic development;
- An influence for the good;
- An inspiration for individuals to achieve their full potential.

We also believe that education has the power to be transformative, not only as a result of its function as a provider of knowledge but in its ability to inspire curiosity and challenge thinking. For all of these reasons, it is important that within our roles as educators we are able to teach to and beyond the curriculum and perhaps some of those added extras are in fact added 'essentials'.

Given the sheer number of things that schools and colleges 'should' be adding into the curriculum, it is impossible to cover everything in a single chapter … and even if we did, we suspect that the text might well be out of date very quickly. The demands on education are not going to ease up soon, so our approach is to work with, rather than against the system but in doing so, be mindful of our own values and beliefs about our roles. For this reason, we have limited the examples in this chapter to key areas that we feel are applicable in all phases of education, these are:

- Developing core skills (literacy, numeracy and using technology);
- Interpersonal skills;
- Wellbeing and resilience.

Developing core skills

Core skills such as literacy, numeracy and using technology are part of everyday life and as such are skills we continue to develop way beyond our formal education – but how can we encourage learners to develop them within other subjects?

Embedding additional skills into a lesson

Imagine you are planning a social science lesson for one of your groups. As part of this you have included the following task:

Research and list the causes of poverty in less developed countries.

How could you embed activities which will also develop literacy and numeracy skills?

There are a range of things you could do but here are a few ideas that you could have used to focus the activity:

- Specify the way you want the learners to present their response. If this is a written response it could be a leaflet, a letter, maybe a poster. Each will involve sentences, punctuation, ordering text and communicating clearly.
- Include the requirement for a graph or image to be part of the answer. This means that numerical information must be included and requires some analytical thinking as well as manipulation of data.
- Consider the task requirements – if you add the requirement to work in pairs or as a group, this will involve discussion and appropriate communication.
- Find ways of giving feedback, individually or to the group as a whole … using skills is one part of the process but developing them means we need to correct mistakes and provide guidance where required.

Literacy skills are essential in all areas of life and most other learning is predicated on our literacy. As a foundation skill, this is something we must pay attention to in every lesson and there are a number of ways we can do this without detracting from the rest of the lesson content. As you can see from the previous activity, when we refer to literacy development it isn't just reading and writing that's important, we should also consider speaking – oracy is also a fundamental skill in life and learning. In our experience, when teachers have grasped the idea of building these additional skills into their lessons, they often find very creative ways of doing so – but if you don't know where to start there are some pointers in Table 8.1.

Table 8.1 Strategies to embed literacy

Strategy	Reading	Writing	Speaking
'What does this mean?' – introduce some text (a paragraph or two) related to the subject. Ask learners to work in pairs. Their task is to read through the text and then rewrite it in fewer than 200 words (you may want to adjust the length of text/rewriting depending on age group and level).	✓	✓	✓
Idea generator – at the beginning of a lesson or as a recap, ask the learners to give you key words or phrases related to the learning. Create a mind map on the Smartboard and ask them to produce their own version.		✓	✓
Completing sentences – using the principle of 'gapped handouts', ask learners to complete sentences related to the topic. This strategy can be paper-based on electronic using a drag a drop facility.	✓	✓	
Shades of meaning – prepare some word cards about key terms/ language related to the topic (this works best with things that learners often confuse or find difficult to define). Ask learners to work in pairs or small groups. You need a set of cards with the terms and another set with two or three definitions (colour coding helps here). The task is to match up the correct sets and then feedback their answers to the rest of the group.	✓		✓
Analysing stories – for this you may use a pertinent short story or an anecdote relating to the subject. Ask learners to work collaboratively to analyse the story and answer some key questions. For example, What is the key message? What are the key stages in the plot? Who are the main protagonists? How does this story relate to your experience?	✓	✓	✓
What's the order? – Find a short piece of text related to the topic, print it and cut it into strips (the size of these will represent level of difficulty ... chunkier strips with more text will be easier than skinny ones), The task is to put the text back in the right order. Go through this as a whole group to check overall understanding of the text – it is also an opportunity to highlight and correct any areas of difficulty.	✓		✓
Teach power words – Every subject has a specialist language attached to it, for example in chemistry we talk about molecules and in history we might refer to a chronicle. To increase fluency in subject-related language create some flashcards. These include the word on one side and the definition on the other. These can be used in a variety of ways ... the key is regularity of use to the point that they are included in sentences with ease.	✓	✓	

Contextualising these 'extra' skills wherever and whenever possible within the subject area enables learners not only relate to them more easily and become more open to their acquisition, but also understand where, when, why and how that they will use them in their everyday life so that they see their relevance. We all use English skills in everyday life when talking to colleagues or learners. We may not use functional maths as often as our oral or written communication skills but think about the ways we use them when we make a trip to the local shop or supermarket. We need to check our change (or receipt), or work out how much that 10 per cent off label is really going to save us and whether buying it is really going to be a bargain – and so will your learners! There are also many ways we can embed numeracy development into other lessons, for example, learners may be asked to look at case studies or reports which contain data that they have to make sense of, perhaps when analysing trends? Perhaps learners could be asked to display information in the form of graphs or when debating something topical they could include data to back up their arguments.

Digital skills

The Realising the Potential of Technology in Education Report by the Department for Education highlighted the fact that, 'Technology has become embedded throughout society and has transformed the way we expect to engage with services and consume content' (DfE, 2019:5). That includes education. Many teachers, particularly those considered to be 'digital natives' (Prensky, 2010) are very familiar with the benefits of information technology and its potential in the educational arena. The same can be said for most learners, but it is important to remember that not everyone is IT 'savvy', so when we want to use new technology in the classroom we need to be prepared for various levels of skill. Things which many of us take for granted – using spreadsheets, making graphs, using PowerPoint, using spell and grammar checkers or even adding attachments to emails can be a challenge for learners unfamiliar with the technology.

We also need to remember that some learners have additional needs and may require adaptations to be made for them to access technology in the classroom (more information on this in Chapter 5). All these elements can, however, be planned into the lesson, for example, when course work or assessments require digital skills for research, collaborating with peers or even submitting work for assessment. Where new digital skills are needed in the classroom, it may be that extra time also has to be planned to allow for learning and practice. Peer support is also invaluable where learners need to expand their digital knowledge and providing opportunities for learners to work together on tasks in groups can be particularly useful in this context. Opportunities for group work can be provided through carefully planning the inclusion of co-operative or collaborative exercises where working with others will both motivate and engage learners in developing digital skills.

Learn from our experience

This anecdote is taken from the experience of one of the authors so is written as a personal reflection.

During the pandemic most, if not all, teachers had to learn a whole new way of teaching to ensure we kept our learners motivated and engaged. We had to learn fast! For me, my first encounter with the new Teams technology for online learning was a disaster. I set up the meeting, invited the learners and then waited, and waited, and waited whilst they managed to get themselves logged on. It was a good 7-10 minutes into the lesson before I had them all there. Then the problems started - problems with cameras and sound malfunctioning were combined with poor internet connections (both my own and the learners!). I tried to share my screen but could not get it to work properly so that it could be seen clearly, and finally, the video I had embedded would not play with sound. I had no idea how to use the chat function, or the hands-up button, breakout groups or the whiteboard. And with no IT support the whole lesson simply fell apart! I felt deflated and demotivated.

As you can see from the previous reflection, teaching with technology can present some challenges, especially for those of us considered to be digital immigrants (Prensky, 2010). But we learnt a lot, not least that teaching with technology requires preparation as well as clear guidance to learners. We soon learnt that starting an online class with some 'rules of engagement' was by far the best way to ensure that everyone followed the same protocols. Practical information such as how to use 'hands up' and chat facilities were just as important as the mechanical considerations such as switching your microphone off when you are not speaking. Even though you are not in the same physical room, learners still rely on their teacher for guidance, especially when a situation is not familiar.

Working with technology undoubtedly has its upside for teaching - it has become easier to incorporate interactive activities, videos, images, mind maps and research activities, and learners are able to access information quickly from a wide range of external sources. It does, however, have its dangers; websites may need to be monitored by teachers and organisations to check the appropriacy of content, and learners may need to be limited in their use of personal mobile technology. Some things which have raised their ugly heads since the inception and mass access to the Internet are cyberbullying, grooming and radicalisation. Various government initiatives have sought to minimise these elements by including the Prevent Strategy (2011) and the raising of awareness of the dangers cyberbullying. An effective way for teachers to support learners in recognising and counteracting these elements can be through the teaching of British values. These include:

- British Value 1 (BV1) - Democracy - based on the principles of freedom and equality, individuals have a right have their views be heard but are aware of their rights and responsibilities.

- British Value 2 (BV2) – The Rule of Law – people should be aware of the reasons for rules and laws and the consequences if these are infringed whilst being responsible for their own actions.
- British Values 3 (BV3) – Individual Liberty – people should be aware that they have rights, freedom of choice and the right to express their opinions, but take responsibility for their behaviour.
- British Value 4 (BV4) – Mutual Respect – individuals should respect the rights of others.
- British Value 5 (BV5) – Tolerance of Those of Different Faiths and Beliefs – individuals should respect the values, ideas and beliefs of others and not try to impose their own views.

These were initially introduced as guidance by the Department for Education (DfE, 2014) and quickly became part of the inspection process carried out by the Office for Standards in Education (Ofsted), with the intention of ensuring the promotion of five values in educational establishments. As with the imperative to include other additions, such as maths, English and digital skills, there can be resistance, especially if they are taught as discrete subjects. However, if discretely included within 'normal' lessons, they are more likely to be accepted and can be contextualised which in turn emphasises their relevance.

Embedding British values

Unlike the other skills mentioned in this chapter, British values are not simply skills to be learnt and used. Often, adopting British values requires a change of mindset so that they become an intrinsic part of everyday behaviour. They are not something which can be acquired through rote learning, instead they require learners to interact with ideas so that previous assumptions might be questioned. To really understand these values, they need to become embedded into everyday life. Once deep learning of the values is achieved, learners will be able to call upon the principles to combat stereotypical thinking and counter arguments when they are presented to them by others or in the media (Sweller et al., 1998).

At first sight the prospect of integrating the values into lesson planning may seem overwhelming but when we look closely at the overall curriculum, there are often naturally occurring opportunities to explore these topics. You may even find you are already embedding a number of values into your current teaching, for example, the use of paired or group work requires us to revisit ideas about respect and democracy. When we set or create rules for classroom activities, we may choose to do this by agreeing what's important. This encourages learners to take ownership of the rules and participating in their compilation means taking part in a democratic process (BV1). We also become aware of our rights and responsibilities in relation to the rules (BV2). It is highly likely that the ground rules set require learners to listen to and respect each other's view (BV4/5), and in co-constructing a set of rules in the first place we are acknowledging individual liberties and the freedom to express opinions (BV3).

As with any activity the discussion phase needs to be carefully monitored by the teacher to ensure that the group stays 'on task' and the process remains inclusive and presents a safe space in which learners can express themselves. Learners may not recognise at first that they are practising and embedding the values in their learning, and it may be necessary for the teacher to remind them occasionally of these and how they are being demonstrated in practice. However, discussions, particularly those dealing with sensitive subject matter, can become heated, leading to the ground rules being ignored and may require the teacher to intervene occasionally to retain task focus and ensure that the BVs are being both implemented and maintained.

Artificial intelligence (AI)

Unless you have been living under a rock or hiding in splendid isolation, there is no doubt, that you will have heard about the explosion in artificial intelligence in the past several months and this, of course, must be included in any discussion about digital skills. Whilst we are aware that something developing at such a rapid rate will quickly go out of date, it is important to outline the general principles.

Despite the current media focus and frenzy on AI, particularly in terms of education, it is important first to note that the presence of AI in the classroom isn't entirely new. We have been using early (albeit primitive) forms of AI for a while in things like quiz apps and support websites. So let yourself be slightly eased by that fact and realise that teachers are not going to be replaced by ChatGPT tomorrow. In fact, if there is one thing that we learned from the pandemic, it is the value of human interaction in teaching and learning. A DfE report from 2022 concluded that during the pandemic, 'online learning was difficult for the young people interviewed; they had found it demotivating and stressful.' (DfE, 2022:28).

Another element that has been the focus of media attention on AI is the idea that learners will start to use AI to cheat. There are learners who will, just in the same way as there are, and always have been, learners who will copy their friend's work and submit it as their own. We have developed guardrails for that through systems like TurnItIn and other plagiarism checkers, which are certainly racing to develop the technology to include new AI tools. Perhaps the most effective guardrail, however, is knowing your students and recognising when a completely flawless piece of work might not be entirely representative of a particular learner and that questions should be asked. You might also consider assessments other than essays or reports – more creative assessments can make plagiarism much more difficult.

Teachers' concerns about AI are very real but perhaps we should also consider some of the potential it offers and how we can leverage AI as a teaching and learning tool. Ironically, ChatGPT gives a pretty good answer to how it can be used in the classroom, so if you aren't sure, just ask it. Some of the real benefits are that AI has the potential to reduce teacher workload by providing learners with real-time feedback on their work, which in turn helps learners draft, modify and improve their work before submission. One of the most encouraging and exciting potential benefits of AI is its ability to provide individualised support and feedback to learners in the way that having a personal tutor or teaching assistant would. Think of the practice of flipped learning; the basic premise is that instead of the traditional model where teachers deliver content and then send learners away to practise application of knowledge by producing homework. The content teaching happens outside of the classroom through videos, workshops or other online activities and the application and practice happens in the classroom where teachers can provide feedback and address misconceptions in real time. AI can provide the potential for that feedback, motivation and correction to happen at any time, on an individual basis. There is the potential for learners to ask probing questions or for AI to mimic a historical figure or character from literature for the learner to converse with, creating deep and meaningful learning experiences. AI can also be really good at Socratic questioning, helping learners to further develop their ideas and consider counter arguments.

If you are particularly interested in applications for AI in technology, you may want to watch of few of the TED Talks posted on the Padlet page. One particular talk to note is Sal Khan's talk; 'How AI Can Save (Not Destroy) Education' (2023). Khan is the founder of Khan Academy, a flipped learning tool that gives learners access to a curated collection of tutorial videos matched with sets of questions designed to teach to mastery (ensuring solid understanding before learners progress). In this talk he explores the range of tools that Khan Academy is developing to enhance learning and understanding, including many of the applications explored above, where learners can ask questions and explore through natural curiosity and discovery and the AI acts like a tutor, not giving the answer, but asking more questions.

There are, of course, a number of ethical considerations teachers need to consider when incorporating AI into the teaching and learning process. AI is still a program and therefore may be subject to the bias of its programmers, which could lead to the 'promotion of certain ideologies without transparency' (Greene-Harper, 2023, online). Data privacy, safeguarding, Prevent and transparency are all concerns central to the development of AI and its use in education. Greene-Harper argues that it is 'imperative to prioritise the ethical use of AI in learning to ensure that it serves the best interests of students and upholds their rights to privacy'.

As the debate about the need for caution and the frightening potential of AI (that comes from nearly any Sci-Fi movie you have ever) seen rages on, consider some key points made by Sal Kahn in his TED Talk. If we demand a pause in the development of AI, only those who follow the rules will pause, and bad actors who wish to use AI for nefarious means such as information control, etc. will continue to develop it. We need, as educators, to be part of the conversation, not bury our heads and let the conversation happen without us. In the words of Khan 'Better we fight for the positive use cases. Perhaps the most poetic use case is if AI (Artificial Intelligence) can be used to enhance HI (Human Intelligence, human potential and human purpose)' (2023, online).

Leveraging learning technology

There are a number of tools that will make it easier for teachers to embed additional curricular elements such as English and maths as starter activities to get learners thinking and settled in the classroom. 'Starter of the day' is a website that does exactly what it says on the tin, there is a maths starter for every day of the year. Sporcle.com (referenced in Chapter 3) has a quiz on nearly anything you can think of so it can be a really valuable tool to help learners explore an infinite range of topics that arise. For example, through discussion you discover that some of your learners did not know the geography of Europe very well, you could find a good quiz on Sporcle and use it as a starter for the next few sessions to help them improve. Quizizz (referenced in Chapters 3 and 6) will also have several game-like quizzes that would work for additional topics.

It is perhaps more valuable to find tools that add tangible value to the main subject you are teaching whilst still developing core skills in other areas. One great tool for this could be Gapminder.org, a website dedicated to 'fighting global misconceptions'. The website is full of teaching resources and materials and has two particularly interesting tools which can be used with students. The first is called the worldview upgrader, where learners take a 13-question quiz designed to assess and highlight misconceptions they have about the world. The other, 'Animating Data', is a great tool for making data about the world around us come alive. It allows you to choose from an amazing range of data sets collected by global organisations such as the United Nations and look at how that data has changed over time and between one nation and another. The data set is broad enough to be relevant to nearly any subject so if you want to know the relationship between life expectancy and cavities per child, you can do that here. Ted.ed.com (and its parent site TED.com) is also an excellent tool for supporting broader learning on any number of topics and allows teachers to easily build a remote or flipped lesson around any video on YouTube, TED Talks or TedEd.

A final consideration is to think about how we teach learners to check information they find online. Modelling how to identify reputable sources is vital to almost all of the additional skills identified in this chapter. One way to start this process could be to consider curating content for learners around a certain topic or working with learners to create a bank of resources they have pre-vetted for each other. Padlet.com and similar tools like Wakelet would be excellent for this, but any virtual learning environment would also let you build a bank or sources for research.

Interpersonal skills

Interpersonal skills is a term bandied around in many settings but rarely defined – everyone thinks they know what the term means but definitions might vary. A bit like 'love' … You know it when you see/feel it but can you articulate an accurate definition for others? In this section we will discuss the interpersonal skills which help facilitate social situations. The nuances of behaviour which help us to navigate everyday life in a positive way. They may include aspects of emotional intelligence (which we will look at in the next section), building relationships, respect and recognising boundaries. Many of the skills outlined here might be considered 'incidental', in that they are often developed through situated (learning that takes place outside of formal structures). In this way, what we learn is seen as the acquisition of knowledge as a result of participation in social interaction (Lave, 1988).

Interpersonal skills

Throughout this chapter (and much of this book) we have looked either directly or indirectly at interpersonal skills. These might be between learners and teachers or learners and peers. Review this chapter (and others if you have the time) and think about how these skills can be brought into play in teaching and learning. Once you have done this think about your own teaching and consider how you could develop interpersonal skills between yourself and your learners and between learners.

Building relationships

Managing and building relationships is one of the most important life skills that we can develop and of course this involves several elements including showing respect for others, teamworking and negotiation. All of these things can be learned during planned activities such as teacher- or student-led discussions, or working as a member of a team researching a specific topic. These activities also provide opportunities to build the personal qualities valued by employers. Indeed it has been argued that employers often appoint people based on how well they will fit into existing teams and many of these skills can be learnt 'incidentally' simply by taking part in a range of activities.

Respecting others and recognising boundaries

When people show a lack of respect it is often as a result of ignorance, rather than a deliberate act. For example, we may visit another country and inadvertently cause offence simply because we are unaware of cultural differences – in Cambodia and Malaysia pointing directly at someone is considered extremely rude, and the 'thumbs up' sign (perfectly acceptable in many countries) is considered inappropriate in Greece and Russia. One way to overcome such mishaps is to encourage open communication about issues of respect and boundaries, particularly if you are teaching a multi-cultural class – and this is most easily achieved when you create a safe space within the classroom, one that is open to discussion and free of judgement. Using Roger's framework about 'unconditional positive regard' is a very good starting point (Rogers, 1961). This doesn't mean we necessarily hold everyone in high esteem, it simply means that we show acceptance of difference. This can be achieved by:

- Encouraging reflection;
- Sharing thoughts and feelings about specific events;
- Considering events from a range of perspectives;
- Showing acceptance of another's views;
- Showing empathy;
- Avoiding judgement (Thompson, 2019).

Emotional intelligence

The theory of emotional intelligence was initially developed through studies of cognition and affect, specifically, exploring how our emotions affect our thoughts and subsequent actions. According to Salovey and Mayer (1990), this is something which can be enhanced through the development of five basic skills:

- Self-awareness – being able to recognise and understand how actions and attitudes can influence others;
- Self-regulation – being able to control actions and attitudes by thinking before speaking or acting;
- Intrinsic motivation – wanting to achieve a goal or achieving a target for personal reasons;
- Empathy – being able to recognise and understand to the actions of other people by 'putting themselves in other's shoes;
- Social skills – being able to manage relationships with others.

These skills are not instantly learnt, they often evolve over time and as with all interpersonal skills are usually learnt in situ. This gives the impression that they are somewhat incidental, but as all good teachers know, the opportunities to develop interpersonal skills are usually built into classroom activities. If you look back at some of the tasks included in Table 8.1, you will see that many of them not only require learners to exercise conventional skills such as reading and writing, they also require problem solving, the use of reasoning, critical evaluation and working effectively with others.

Wellbeing and mental health

The World Health Organisation describes wellbeing as 'A positive state experienced by individuals and societies [which encompasses] quality of life and the ability of people and societies to contribute to the world with a sense of meaning and purpose' (World Health Organization, 2021:10). Doesn't that also describe how an individual should flourish in a well organised classroom?

Bronfenbrenner (2005) in his ecological theory describes the systems of interaction in which individuals exist and which affect individual wellbeing. Learners learn within the microsystem of the classroom through interaction with staff and other learners in an environment which is influenced by external systems such as community, societal beliefs and government actions. The past few years have seen a considerable challenge to wellbeing in the form of the pandemic which disrupted normal education in so many ways, an unprecedented situation imposing new and unfamiliar forms of teaching and learning. The continuing effect of this on the general wellbeing of learners cannot be ignored and is certainly something to be recognised by teachers.

Throughout this book we have looked at different ways in which planning for teaching can indirectly support student wellbeing. Self-acceptance and growth can be developed by carefully scaffolding support to enable learners to move from the known to the unknown in a challenging but non-threatening fashion. Mastery skills can be developed through the careful selection of activities which embed deeper learning and encourage critical thinking and self-efficacy. Positive relationships with peers which can be fostered through group activities help to generate a sense of belonging. Thoughtful planning allows us to create a learning environment in which all learners can flourish.

Embedding and interleaving

Many of the strategies mentioned in this chapter are based on the principle of embedding additional skills. By this we mean implanting new learning within a given context ... another way of looking at it might be 'hiding'. When we teach additional things such as English, maths or using technology by including them in activities related to a subject, we are in fact hiding them within the main topic. The reason for this is that we want learners to focus on the subject content, not least because that's what they think they should be learning. That said, many teachers are quite explicit about the additional skills they are incorporating within a lesson or within a given activity. This is very much a personal decision and one you will be best placed to make once you get to know your learners.

Another strategy used to incorporate additional skills is that of interleaving. This is where we might deliberately mix together subjects in order to enhance learning. So, instead of a block of learning focussed on a particular topic, the teacher covers several topics at a time so that learners need to switch their attention for new activities. This doesn't mean that topics are totally unrelated – if you were to use history as an example, rather than learning about the full history of a country and moving on, this could be mixed up by looking at histories of other countries, different parts of history from each country could be interleaved based around a common theme. By regularly reintroducing similar content or tasks, learners are forced to draw comparisons, which in turn should support retention of the material. The rationale behind this is that learners are reinforcing their learning through related activities but also have to discriminate between concepts.

Summary

In this chapter we have looked at areas which although integral to the teaching process are not always seen as being a major part of the curriculum. When there has been pressure to teach these as discrete subjects there has frequently been resistance from both staff and learners who have seen them as tangential to the main programme. They are, however, an important part of the curriculum whether hidden or interwoven into other topics as they prepare learners, not only for success in their education, but in life.

References

Bronfenbrenner, U. (2005) *Making Human Beings Human: Bioecological Perspectives on Human Development*. Thousand Oaks, CA: Sage Publications Inc.

Burke, M. and Lehain, M. (2018) 'Clogging up the Classroom: The Jostle for Curriculum Content'. Available at: https://parentsandteachers.org.uk/wp-content/uploads/2019/03/20181221_-_WSST_-_Clogging_up_the_classroom.pdf [Accessed 19/5/23]

Dearing R (1997) *National Committee of Inquiry into Higher Education*. Available at www.educationengl and.org.uk/documents/dearing1997/dearing1997.html [Accessed 21 April 2023].

DfE (2014) *Guidance on promoting British values in schools*. Available at: www.gov.uk/government/news/guidance-on-promoting-british-values-in-schools-published [Accessed 21 April 2023].

DfE (2019) *Realising the Potential of Technology in Education* Available at: www.gov.uk/government/publications/realising-the-potential-of-technology-in-education [Accessed 21 April 2023].

DfE (2022) '*16*-19 Learners' Experiences of the Covid-19 Pandemic', *Family, Kids and Youth*. Available at: https://assets.publishing.service.gov.uk/government/uploads/system/uploads/attachment_data/file/1074701/16_to_19_learners__experiences_of_the_COVID-19_pandemic.pdf [Accessed 5 June 2023].

Gov.UK (2011) *Prevent Strategy 2011/* Available at: http://Prevent strategy 2011 – GOV.UK (www.gov.uk) [Accessed 21 April 2023].

Greene-Harper, R. (2023) *The Pros and Cons of Using AI in Learning: Is ChatGPT Helping of Hindering Learning Outcomes?* ELearning Industry. [online] Available at: https://elearningindustry.com/pros-and-cons-of-using-ai-in-learning-chatgpt-helping-or-hindering-learning-outcomes [Accessed 5 June 2023].

Khan, S. (2023) *How AI and Save (Not Destroy) Education*. [video online] Available at: www.ted.com/talks/sal_khan_how_ai_could_save_not_destroy_education [Accessed 5 June 2023].

Lave, J. (1988) *Cognition in Practice: Mind, Mathematics, and Culture in Everyday Life*. Cambridge: Cambridge University Press.

Prensky, M, (2010) *Teaching Digital Natives: Partnering for Real Learning*. Thousand Oaks, California: Corwin Press.

Rogers, C. R. (1961) *On Becoming a Person: A Psychotherapist's View of Psychotherapy*. London: Constable and Robinson Ltd.

Salovey, P. and Mayer, J. D. (1990) 'Emotional Intelligence', *Imagination, Cognition and Personality*, 9(3), 185–211.

Sweller, J., van Merrienboer, J. J. G. and Paas, F. G. W. C. (1998) 'Cognitive Architecture and Instructional Design', *Educational Psychology Review*, 9(10), 251–342.

Thompson, C (2019) *The Magic of Mentoring: Developing Others and Yourself*, Oxon: Routledge.

Tomlinson, R. (2004) *14-19 Curriculum and Qualifications Reform Final Report of the Working Group on 14-19 Reform*. Available at: https://webarchive.nationalarchives.gov.uk/ukgwa/20050301194752/http://www.dfes.gov.uk/14-19/documents/Final%20Report.pdf [Accessed 21 April 2023].

World Health Organization (2021) '*Health Promotion Glossary of Terms*', Available at: 9789240038349-eng.pdf (who.int) [Accessed: 24 October 2023].

9 Concluding the lesson

Introduction

It was the end of the lesson. I asked the usual question 'Anyone got any questions?' and got the usual non-response from the students who were beginning to fidget, surreptitiously packing their books into their backpacks and obviously itching to pick up where they left off with their pre-lesson chats. Well, I had tried to make sure they understood what the lesson was about, it was planned and taught the way I intended and I covered all the information that I needed to. They worked a bit in groups, but they are a noisy bunch, so I don't let them do too much of this or they go off topic very quickly. I got the usual 'Bye Miss', 'See you next week Miss', 'Have a nice weekend Miss', as they disappeared out of the classroom *en route* to their lesson, lunch or whatever was next, but had they really learned everything that I had set out to teach them? Nobody asked any questions, so can I take that as an indicator that they all took everything in? Will they remember it for next time? How can I find out?

This is a journal entry from a trainee teacher – does it seem familiar? We have all been in this situation – put our heart and souls into teaching, spent hours planning, working out different strategies and researching ways of engaging learners. Nonetheless, just like the example above, at some point we have all had that nagging feeling at the end of a lesson – the one that says, 'I'm not sure they really understood what I was teaching'. So, what can we do as to find out not only what has been learned but also what hasn't? The answer lies in how we organise the conclusion to our lesson. Too often, this is the 'poor relation' in terms of teaching and learning, pulled in hurriedly at the end of a lesson and not really serving much of a purpose other than as a signal to the group that it is time to pack up. But just like Oliver Twist, concluding lessons deserve 'more'. 'More' in terms of planning, more in terms of content and more for you as the teacher in terms of helping you to identify the level and amount of learning that has taken place. We would also suggest that the end of the lesson should contain more for the learners so that they might reflect on what they have accomplished. In this chapter we will look at how we can develop the conclusion or lesson plenary to give us more.

DOI: 10.4324/9781003385905-10

The plenary

Before planning plenaries, it is essential that we understand what it is and why we are doing it. The word plenary is bandied around in teaching, but what does it actually mean? At its simplest a plenary is a meeting that everyone has the right to attend, so in terms of teaching, all those involved in the lesson, learners, teachers and learning support staff, have a right to participate. Meetings which have any value are those which have a purpose and the same applies to plenaries used in teaching and learning. In a classroom context the plenary session has taken on the specialised purpose of evaluating learning, so its primary focus is on the learners and their progress (or lack thereof!). Okay, we have established that all students have a right to participate in the plenary but how do we make sure that we evaluate the level of learning achieved by *all* learners and not just a few?

In earlier chapters of this book, we looked at aims and objectives for the lesson - planning the journey we intended our learners to travel, where they were going to finish and how they were going to get there. Part of the purpose of planning an effective plenary to conclude the lesson is to determine which learners have arrived safely at the learning destination and identify those who may have 'got lost' on the way. By using the plenary to find out when and where they got lost the teacher can start a 'rescue mission' either by taking action there and then, or by planning to review and retrace the pathway in subsequent lessons to enable them find their way to the learning objective.

Activity

The previous example shows the importance of having a plenary, but it doesn't tell the whole story. Think about other possible reasons why lessons should be concluded with an effective plenary - and write down as many as you can think of.

In trying to assess whether your learners 'arrived safely' at the learning destination, you may have listed some or any of the following:

- It gives teachers feedback on progress.
- It helps learners develop a stronger bond with previous learning or existing knowledge.
- It allows teachers to summarise and review the lesson, which will help learners identify and retain key information.
- It can help to create links to the next lesson.
- It encourages learners to ask questions and clarify their understanding.
- It can confirm links between ideas and theories.
- It can help teachers to decide what needs to be taught next.
- It allows learners to discuss their thoughts with their peers as well as the teacher.

Planning the plenary

As Hattie (2012) suggests, the plenary allows teachers to review the lesson and the learning through their learners' eyes, enabling the teacher to assess the impact of the lesson and check that they are in a position to move forward. Plenaries are not just 'something that happens', they need to be planned into the lesson in same way as other activities and time allowed for them to be carried out effectively so that issues that could impact on homework, assignments and motivation are addressed. However, as with all the best laid plans there needs to be some flexibility. As lessons progress learners' needs may change depending on their understanding of the topic. It may, therefore, be necessary to change the lesson plan, by reviewing the learning process and perhaps inserting additional information to reinforce current understandings or extend the knowledge base. The length of time spent on a plenary cannot therefore be totally prescriptive, its duration must be relative to the amount and type of learning to be checked. The important message here is to make sure you leave some time in the plan overall, otherwise the end of the lesson could be very rushed.

Involving students

Fortunately, the days of strict teacher control and didactic methods are long behind us and today's learner-centred classrooms involve a range of methods which promote inter-action between teacher and learners. Learners are (and expect to be) actively involved in the lesson and the plenary is no exception. Therefore, unlike the example at the beginning of this chapter, when planning a plenary we need to consider strategies which will not only consolidate learning but will also involve all learners.

Strategies for plenaries

Deciding which strategy to use when planning the plenary is a bit of a 'horses for courses' decision. The runners and riders are many and various, but whether they actually take part in a race is often determined by the conditions or context. It's no good asking a horse bred for flat racing to take part in a steeplechase – the skill set (galloping fast) which they have learned and practised is incompatible with the need for them to jump obstacles, and all that is likely to happen is that horse and jockey will come to grief in some way. In a similar way you have a choice about which method you use in the plenary, but it must be the right one otherwise the plenary will fail to meet the objective of accurately assessing learning.

Learn from our experience

One of the most interesting parts of working in teacher education is watching students practice teaching *in situ*. The following is from an observation report on a teacher in training:

The lesson topic was 'different types of bonds used in brickwork'. The trainee teacher, having spent more than the allocated time to the instruction element of teaching, hurriedly moved on to conclude the lesson by asking one question – 'What have you learned today?' This received only one response, 'Something about bonds' – and with that, the class was dismissed.

How effective was the plenary in that lesson? Did it provide the teacher (or learners) with any tangible information on what had been learnt? To check the learning for this lesson (or any other practical activity), it might have been more appropriate to ask the learners to describe something specific, so in this case, a specific type of bond. Or perhaps it would be useful to ask for a demonstration of learning by actually creating a bond? Both might work well but which you choose to use will depend on what it is that you are trying to assess. Description may indicate theoretical knowledge, whereas a practical demonstration can indicate understanding and application of learning.

Checking surface learning

At the beginning of any new subject it is important to lay the foundations for later development by learning core concepts within a subject. This is a bit like taking 'baby steps' towards understanding in that we learn the fundamentals first. The fundamentals might be something like a definition or key terms, and when we ask our learners to demonstrate their understanding of this they might simply state the answer without any further elaboration. This response demonstrates their ability to recall information; however, it does not demonstrate any further understanding and by asking for a simple response we are simply checking surface learning. You may remember this idea from Chapter 7; when we talk about surface learning, we are referring to information we have accepted as important and simply memorised without question. We might check this by using strategies such as question and answer or online quizzes. This is entirely appropriate at the early stages as being able to respond accurately not only provides an opportunity for reinforcement, it also gives learners more confidence in their learning.

Checking deep learning

Shanahan (2005) argues that understanding is an active process requiring interpretation of new knowledge or information, so that it can be assimilated and in turn applied to different situations. As we discussed in Chapter 7, one way of achieving this is through the use of collaborative or co-operative group work, which provides the opportunity for exploring ideas through research and discussion. It also offers a framework for reviewing and clarifying learning, which in turn aids comprehension and leads to a deeper understanding of the topic. This approach is also something which can be used effectively in a plenary by asking each group or pair to present their findings for analysis and discussion. However, as we outlined in Chapter 5, not every learner responds well to group work. This doesn't mean we shouldn't use it, it simply means we can't rely on it. In Table 9.1 we have outlined some alternative strategies for higher level learning that may work well in plenaries and provides some examples of simple strategies you can use if you want to include some 'lower level' checks.

Table 9.1 Deep and surface learning strategies

Deep learning

Strategy description	Purpose
Peer to peer teaching – learners work in pairs and teach each other a chosen element of the lesson. The pairs can be switched around so that each plays the role of teacher and learner.	Forces the 'teacher' to break down the learning so that it can be taught in a logical way and provides the opportunity for the 'learner' to ask specific questions. Learning is reinforced through repetition.
Creating mind maps – learners can work individually, in pairs or in groups and create a mind map of what they have learnt in the lesson.	Highlights connections between elements of the learning and shows where there are gaps in what has been remembered. Mind maps can be revisited at the start of the next lesson.
Socratic questioning – learners can work in pairs and create questions about the lesson content using the Socratic approach.	This provides an opportunity to explore any assumptions and encourages thinking about what has been learnt in a critical way. An outline of the question types can be found in Chapter 6.
Connecting concepts – this is a whole group activity completed on a whiteboard (or large sheet of paper). The teacher starts by asking for a volunteer to write up a key word or phrase linked to their learning. Then others are asked to add to the concept map, showing how their learning connects to the first item.	This requires an understanding of how different elements of learning link together and provides an opportunity for learners to ask questions about any links they don't understand. Figure 9.1 shows how this might look in practice.
Applying learning – small group, paired or individual activity to identify situations or contexts in which the lesson content could be applied.	This encourages learners to think about the how and where learning can be applied to explain situations or contexts to develop their skills in transferring knowledge.

Surface learning

Strategy description	Purpose
Identify 3 things – learners work individually to identify 3 facts or terms which are new to them and either write them on post-its before putting them on the board or sending them to a Padlet if IT is available.	Learners have to reflect on the lesson and identify and recall information. Allows the teacher to check that learners have identified the key elements being taught.
Labelling – learners work together to match labels of key terms or words to areas on a diagram.	This requires the learners to begin to apply their learning and encourages recall.
Complete a crossword – meanings or descriptions of key elements of learning are used as clues to specific terms. Learners have to complete the crossword using the correct terms.	Learners have to make connections between words and meaning.
Demonstration – learners have to demonstrate each stage of a learned skill.	Tests accuracy of recall and allows both learners and teacher to identify any areas of difficulty which need to be addressed quickly and easily.

Table 9.1 (Continued)

Surface learning	
Strategy description	**Purpose**
Building mnemonics – teacher provides the key words or terms used in the lesson – working in groups learners have to devise a mnemonic to remember the terms.	Everyone has their own way of remembering things and this encourages learners to find their own ways to recall information. Be warned – if you employ this method some of the mnemonics might be a bit rude!

Affective learning	
Strategy description	**Purpose**
Journal entry – an individual activity to write down their thoughts and fears.	Learners identify what they feel confident that have understood and areas where they feel that they are struggling.
Emojis – emoji feedback sheets are distributed and learners circle those that they feel apply to them before writing a 1 or 2 sentence commentary.	Learners are encouraged to indicate their feelings as emojis and then explore these in writing to identify areas where they feel they may need further help or advice.
Motivators – written or oral activity that allows learners to identify one activity of resource which has motivated them to participate in the lesson.	Highlights different motivators within the group and can be helpful with planning future learning activities.
Two stars and a wish – learners write down two things that went well in the lesson with a wish about what they want to achieve in the next lesson.	Learners reflect on their learning identifying areas of strength and areas for development.

The importance of retrieval practice

You may recall that we introduced the idea of retrieval practice in Chapter 3 and provided an overview of how this theory works in practice. The benefits of retrieving information from the memory are widely acknowledged as an effective technique for improving recall (Carpenter and Delosh, 2005; Argawal et al., 2016), and although originally seen as a form of testing, retrieval practice actually improves knowledge acquisition which may be transferred to a range of contexts (Roediger and Butler, 2010). In its simplest form this is about finding an answer to a question by retrieving information from the memory, and this is something we are very likely to do within a plenary. This may be achieved by question and answer but could also include a number of other activities such as the group activities mentioned earlier, or question sheets, using flash cards, perhaps even completing tests. You could even consider a 'pub quiz' to be an experience of retrieval practice! Although that may be less relevant for your learners (unless you teach in post-compulsory education). As we have mentioned previously, part of the process of developing deep learning is the transfer of information from the short-term to the long-term memory. Retrieval is an active process, requiring a cognitive effort which helps consolidate learning and helps us to make connections with previously learned information. Therefore, it is something we need to practise, and incorporating retrieval practice into a plenary is not only sensible, it is essential.

Signposting

As we suggested at the beginning of this chapter, one of the key purposes of plenaries is to provide feedback on learning that has taken place in the lesson, but we need to remember that the plenary isn't just a signal for the end of the lesson, it is also a bridge to the next. To bridge effectively, it is important to make the connection between the current lesson and the next. This gives learners a taste of what's to come and shows the overall connectivity in the subject.

In bridging we are aiming to achieve two things, the first is to provide insight into how current learning fits into intended learning, in effect showing that all lessons are connected and should not be seen in isolation. The second aim is to encourage transfer of learning. You will remember in Chapter 7 that we discussed ideas about near and far transfer; near referring to situations where there is some overlap and far when we are transferring learning to a new situation. Either may apply, depending on how your curriculum is organised, but the key point here is that by encouraging transfer of learning you are also supporting learners to develop deep rather than surface approaches. Some strategies you could use to achieve this within a plenary include:

- Considering possible applications of learning – perhaps by asking learners where they might be able to use what they have learnt in the lesson?
- Encouraging generalisation – here you might ask learners to draw out key principles of the learning and again link those to different scenarios where the learning might be useful.
- Requesting reflection – this encourages learners to monitor and evaluate their own thinking and you can prompt this by seeking a 'backward reaching transfer', for example, what does today's lesson remind you of? What strategies have you used before that have helped you in similar learning? Alternatively, this could take the form of a 'forward-reaching transfer' by asking for reflections on what went well or less well and how might this learning be used elsewhere?

Bridging

What strategies could you use to create a bridge from the current lesson to the next? Try to test your imagination by thinking of five different approaches. Get creative and think about things which will make sure your learners are looking forward to the next instalment.

Figure 9.1 Bridge

Leveraging learning technology

In the preceding chapters we have explored a wide variety of tools that would work well as plenary activities, but as suggested in this chapter, choosing the right one is vital if you want to get useful information for future planning.

Many of the tools that teachers use most regularly as plenaries – things like Kahoot, Quizizz or Blooket, are really intended to assess surface knowledge and therefore are best for use in the early stages of learning new material. They are perfect for reviews at the beginning of a unit or as initial assessments, but for deeper learning, there are more appropriate tools. Here you might consider something that requires learners to explain or demonstrate their understanding. Flipgrid.com (a Microsoft partner) is a website and companion app that allows teachers to set questions to which learners can respond via a video between 30 seconds and 10 minutes in length. Teachers can allow learners to modify and edit their videos with filters and stickers, to use sound only or even to see and comment on other submissions. Think about the brickwork class we talked about earlier – the teacher could have asked the learners to work in pairs to create a short video demonstration on a type of bond, or they could discuss where a certain type of bonding might be used.

Any of the tools we have explored which require learners to create content would provide an opportunity to reflect on and evaluate learning. They could also be used as part of a peer assessment activity. For example, many art teachers use Padlet as a tool for learners to peer critique. Learners simply post their work on a Padlet throughout the session and the group offers feedback to one another as part of the plenary activity. Microsoft and Google classrooms both offer functionality that could be used in a similar way.

It is quite common for new teachers to run short on time at the end of the session, so having a bank of ideas (whether they involve ILT or not) is often helpful.

Summary

In this chapter we have considered the importance of concluding lessons in a way which motivates both teachers and learners to reflect on what learning has taken place. Concluding the lesson need not be the poor relation to other aspects of planning; it should not be a rushed, often absent, part of our planning. It is, in fact, a summary, an evaluation and a bridge and should be treated with the respect it deserves.

References

Argawal, P. K., Finlay, J. R., Rose, N. S. and Roediger, H. (2016) 'Benefits from Retrieval Practice Are Greater for Students with Lower Working Memory Capacity', *Memory*, 25(6), 764-771.

Carpenter, S. K. and DeLosh, E. L. (2005) 'Application of the Testing and Spacing Effects To Name Learning', *Applied Cognitive Psychology*, 19, 619-636.

Hattie, J. (2012) *Visible Learning for Teachers: Maximising Impact on Learning*. Abingdon: Routledge.

Roediger, H. L. and Butler, A. C., (2010) 'The Critical Role of Retrieval Practice in Long-Term Retention', *Trends in Cognitive Sciences*, 15(1), 20-27.

Shanahan, T. (2005) *The National Reading Panel Report: Practical Advice for Teachers*. Naperville, IL: Learning Point Associates.

10 Evaluating the lesson

Introduction

'What is this life if, full of care, we have no time to stand and stare?' (Davis, 1911:online) This well-known poem highlights how modern life, full to the brim with daily activities, has distanced us from nature. In essence, we have: 'No time to see, in broad daylight, streams full of stars, like skies at night' – and, as a result, may be missing the beauty in simplicity. In most professional roles, every minute of the working day is scheduled with some sort of activity, making is seem impossible to stop and reflect. What is interesting is the date of the original poem – a time before the internet, mobile technology and a constant stream of information. If time was precious then, now it is like the Holy Grail! In this chapter we will consider the importance of taking the time to evaluate lessons as well as reflect on professional practice, and in doing so challenge our perspectives, provide scope for deeper learning and maybe even transform our thinking!

Why should you reflect?

Reflecting on practice may provide us with the platform to develop new ideas. By looking at what goes well and less well we begin to work in a more objective way. Through honest reflection we are able to develop a level of self-awareness that allows us to critically examine assumptions, as well as our responses to events. If we do this in a structured way we increase our ability to find clarity, which in turn leads to new ways of thinking. But why is this important? It is likely that you have already thought through your lesson, considered the best approaches and made sure you checked whether or not learning was happening … why do you need to think about it all over again? To answer this question we need look no further than Milne's classic *Winnie the Pooh* (Figure 10.1). Dragged along by Christopher Robin, Edward Bear descends the stairs: 'it is, as far as he knows, the only way of coming downstairs, but sometimes he feels there really is another way. If only he could stop bumping for a moment and think of it' (Milne, 1926:1). Once we are embedded into a professional role, most of us spend our days 'bumping along' without questioning what we are doing or how we are doing it. Perhaps this is because of the power of routine or maybe because we feel we don't have the space to think about how we might do things differently. It is even possible that we are simply happy with the way things are? All well and good, but without some form

DOI: 10.4324/9781003385905-11

Figure 10.1 Bump bump bump

of evaluation of what we do, practice becomes a treadmill – we have continuous motion but we may not be travelling anywhere.

Reflection takes time and very often this is scarce. The priority is teaching, preparation, meetings, marking ... when the lesson ends, we go on to something else. By taking the time to reflect we may find that we discover more effective approaches, different ways of thinking, even time efficiencies, and we can do this by spending a very small amount of our day in reflection.

Ways of reflecting on practice

There is often an assumption that reflection is an innate ability, something we are wired to do like our ability to develop language. We only need to look at stages of cognitive development (Piaget, 1957) to see that thinking in a reflective way develops as early as the pre-operational state (where children develop memory, imagination and can understand the ideas of past and future). Reflection is embedded within these activities. We reflect on past events and we imagine what they might look like in the future; in this way it is a very natural part of the thinking process. However, when we reflect on our professional activities, we do this within tight time constraints, often focussing attention on things we consider to be problems for which we must seek solutions – certainly a useful process (and something we should build into our practice) but it isn't the whole story. This type of thinking may drive us to focus on goals that fix a particular issue but won't necessarily bring fresh insights, creative solutions or greater awareness. For this, we need to build our reflective capacity to what Dewey terms 'thinking well' – a process which provides the opportunity to unpick events by avoiding simplistic deductions and encouraging critical examination. Whilst this may not provide the immediate solutions often encouraged in 'quick-fix' cultures, it does provided the opportunity for deliberate thought and that should come with a word of warning. Deliberate thinking can be challenging as: 'it involves overcoming the inertia that inclines one to accept suggestions at their face value; it involves willingness to endure a condition of mental unrest and disturbance' (Dewey 1910:10).

The power of routine

Although 'bumping along' with day-to-day routines can be limiting for our practice, there are times when habit it very useful. This is certainly the case when trying to establish a reflective approach. Establishing small manageable habits is helpful when you want to embed a new behaviour into daily practice, and there are lots of examples where this approach has led to success; Anthony Trollope, used to write in short bursts of 15 minutes, several times a day, every day. This was a routine that was undertaken as a matter of course and one which led to the publication of 47 novels, non-fiction books and a number of articles. There is certainly positive power in embedding routines! Using routine allows us to take incremental steps towards our goals and reflection is no exception. With this in mind, the first step to effective evaluation of your practice is to build a routine around your current activities. This may seem daunting when you already have a busy schedule, but there are ways of easing the pressure so that the new habit becomes almost seamless. The following five steps might help:

1. Decide what your new habit will be (e.g. use a model of critical reflection to evaluate my professional practice).
2. Create some simple and realistic rules to follow – try to base these on something that makes the new habit less of a habit (e.g. I will journal for 10 minutes when I drink my morning coffee).
3. Identify a cue – this helps you stick to the habit (in this example, the cue is making coffee, whilst it is brewing you could get out/log on to your journal).
4. Establish a pre-habit ritual as this will help with the transition between activities. So if you are working before your coffee break, create a ritual to switch the activities (perhaps putting on some music or moving to a different space).
5. Create the right environment – make the new ritual pleasant and easy to adopt.

The key to establishing your new habit it setting it up so that you can't fail.

Choose a model

We don't necessarily advocate sticking to a particular model for reflection, but this may be helpful if you find it difficult to get started. One of the issues here is that there are so many models to choose from and they all have something to recommend them.

Figure 10.2 highlights some popular models (there are many more to choose from should you want to explore a little more). Of the ones we have selected there are some common principles:

- Reflection is usually focussed on a specific experience.
- Reflection may involve acknowledging and examining feelings.
- The steps taken are intended to raise awareness of events and of our own role in events.
- The model should provide the opportunity to view the event from a range of perspectives.
- There is space to make sense of experiences and consider alternative actions.

The idea of 'lenses' for reflection is described very neatly in Brookfield's well-known model in which he recommends looking at an event from different viewpoints (Brookfield, 2017):

- The autobiographical lens – a self-reflection based on our personal experience of an event. This may include considering our own actions and examining our feelings.
- Students' views – whereby we consider how the event might be seen by others. For this lens we would have to take a step back from the central role in the reflection and consider how the event might be experienced by students.
- Colleagues' views – similar to the previous step in that we must try to remove ourselves from the picture and view it from colleagues' perspectives. What would their view be? How might they have handled the situation? What different skills and abilities would they bring to the scene?
- Theoretical lens – in which we would consult literature which allows further analysis of the event. In this we can consider our unique experience in relation to a range of other views. This may mean we can 'normalise' the event (it is highly likely that some part of it relates to some theoretical perspective or other), and we also may be provided with some information which inspires ideas about new things to try.

Reflection and introspection

As already discussed, when we reflect, we are usually considering a particular event from a range of perspectives in order to establish as objective an account as possible. This is a useful process in any professional role and inevitably it will involve exploring how we feel about what has happened. Introspection is a little more personal in that it involves looking inwards by analysing our own thoughts and feelings – we do this in reflection too of course, so it is fair to say the boundaries are blurred. The key difference is where we focus. Often reflection on professional practice is focussed on evaluation and improvement, whereas introspection might be considered more ego-centric, in that its main aim is to develop self-awareness. This can provide a very useful source of personal knowledge which, when done effectively, provides the scope to make connections between experiences, as well as analyse our response to them. This is also very useful in our professional role, particularly if we find ourselves responding in the same (perhaps unproductive) way to triggering events.

A key aim of this type of analysis is that the process will allow us to think about things in different ways which in turn may challenge any unhelpful patterns as well as help to

ERA Cycle (Jasper 2013) like Boud et al. considers three stages to reflection:

- Experience
- Reflection
- Action

Through the Looking Glass (Bolton 2001) focusses on reflexivity and is based on 3 foundations:

- Certain uncertainty
- Serious playfulness
- Unquestioning questioning

Has a focus on trust in the reflective process/ Socratic approach to questioning.

Schön Reflection in action – Reflection on action (1991) – reflection that happens during an event (reflection in action) considering the experience itself and deciding how to act, and reflection that happens after an event (reflection on action) – consideration theoretical perspectives and what you might do differently next time.

Brookfield's Lenses (2017) Analyses a situation using 4 different lenses:

- Self (how do I view the situation?)
- Students (how might students see this?)
- Peers (what might my colleagues think of this?)
- Theoretical perspective (what does the literature say?)

Some key principles in these models:

Reflection usually relates to an experience

Raises awareness of events

Provides the opportunity to view different perspectives

May involve acknowledging and examining feelings

Makes sense of experiences

May lead to further investigation and learning

Increases self-awareness

Provides a basis for change

Considers alternative actions

Mezirow Transformative Learning (1997) - This model is based on the practice of critically evaluating assumptions -'frames of reference' which inform viewpoints and introduced the notion of disorientating dilemmas, events which may prompt a change in our frames of reference. This model includes experience, deep reflection, questioning and reviewing.

Boud et al. Triangular Representation (1985) highlights the link between reflection and learning and contains 3 simple stages:

- Experience
- Reflection
- Learning.

Kolb's Experiential Learning Cycle (1984) includes:

- Concrete experience (what happened)
- Reflection observations (reflections on events)
- Abstract conceptualisation (what does it mean?)
- Active experimentation (what else could I do?)

Atkins and Murphy Cycle (1993) - avoid superficial responses to events. Includes the following stages:

- Awareness
- Description of situation
- Analysis of feelings and knowledge
- Evaluation of relevance
- Identification of learning

Gibbs Reflective Cycle (1998) A cycle approach which contains 6 stages:

- Description
- Feelings
- Evaluation
- Analysis
- Conclusion
- Action plan

John's (2000) Model of Structured Reflection includes:

- Aesthetics (the art of what we do)
- Personal (self-awareness)
- Ethics (moral knowledge)
- Empirics (scientific knowledge)

Also considers reflexivity, taking into account connections with previous experience.

Figure 10.2 Models of reflection

Source: Adapted from Thompson, 2022

consider different approaches. At a superficial level, this should be very simple to do – it is, if we are aware of the potential pitfalls.

Confirmation bias

A common barrier to change is confirmation bias. This is the tendency to interpret things in ways which confirm already held beliefs. It is a cognitive bias that can distort events by the way we think about them. It is very easy to spot this trait in others … when they appear to have 'selective' memories or when they focus on some aspects of a situation (usually the ones which support their current beliefs) and ignore others. There are several types of confirmation bias that you may come across:

- Biased attention – we are selective about what we focus on and may hone in on things which confirm our views whilst paying scant attention, or even ignoring, things that don't. You might notice this when reflecting on something you have just learnt. Suddenly it seems to underpin every other part of your practice and you were just not aware of it. For one of us, that was the discovery of Illeris' Tension Field of Learning (Illeris, 2009). Once learnt, it seemed to underpin every other learning theory. If you haven't experienced this in a professional context, you most certainly will have when you are thinking about buying a new car. What happens once you decide on the make and model? Yes … you see them everywhere!
- Biased interpretation is when we consciously interpret information so that it confirms our beliefs. If you are trying to make a case for how successful (or not) something is, you might well do this, perhaps by selecting aspects of feedback which represent what you want to hear.
- Biased memory is when we remember selectively, holding on to memories which support our views and choosing to forget those which don't.

Potential barriers to reflection

Confirmation bias certainly represents a barrier to reflection that is introspective in nature but what of that which is more evaluative in nature, which is very firmly focussed on our work rather than ourselves (in as much as we can separate the two)? Such barriers can be internal or external in nature. The internal ones are based on previous experiences, so could be the beliefs we hold or the habitual ways in which we have learnt to think about our experience. There are also barriers which come from our environment and sometimes from other people.

Learn from our experience

This except is taken from one of our journals so is written in the first person.

> I have always understood the power of taking time to reflect on life. It may be a result of my upbringing – I was part of a large family where there was always

some sort of drama happening. As the youngest I wasn't usually included in the conversation and was often left to my own devices and would spend most of my time deeply engrossed in a book. Reading took me away from the family drama to different places, different families, different ways of being, and inevitably this began to inform how my own thinking developed. Reading was a gateway to new things and exciting ideas, it inspired me and I often couldn't wait to get my ideas down on paper.

In later years, I felt very privileged to work with trainee teachers who were embarking on their own thinking journeys. I relished sharing my ideas with them, we talked about how to reflect on practice, considered models and talked through keeping a journal. I assumed that like me, my students would welcome the opportunity to reflect and was puzzled when their questions suggested otherwise:

'I don't know how to do my journal'

'As we discussed.. the format is entirely up to you, perhaps you could look at one of the models we discussed?'

'Yeah OK ... but what should I write?'

'How about starting with your thoughts and feelings about what has happened in your placement?'

'OK but what should I write about? I have looked at the assessment criteria and there is nothing there to tell me what you want? And it doesn't say how many words I need?'

(adapted from Thompson, 2022:68-69)

This story illustrates a very common error in teaching and in reflection. That of making assumptions. In assuming that the learners were as enthusiastic about reflection as the teacher, some fundamental points had been missed. The purpose of reflection had not been made clear, so the learners simply saw it as a task they had to complete and wanted to know what they had to do to pass.

Focussing on outcome

As illustrated in the previous story, when we are too focussed on outcomes we may miss out on learning from the process. This is very understandable when we all work under time constraints and feel under pressure to evidence productive use of time. This is something which may lead to a 'sticking plaster' approach, in that, we are aware of an issue and immediately seek a solution, without considering all the options. In addition, if we work in an organisation where we feel that there are high levels of surveillance, for example through lesson observations, or learning walks, this can lead to a culture of being constantly busy, whereby seeking a quick solution becomes a necessity rather than a choice. You may have come across Foucault's ideas of the Panopticon, which is a surveillance tower in a prison environment (Foucault, 1977) – although it is not possible to observe what all of the prisoners are doing all of the time, they don't actually know that, so they self-regulate their activities, resulting in a constant state of activity, with little time to reflect.

Critical thinking

Our habits of thinking have developed over a period of time and are often based on assumptions we have accepted as being correct. Assumptions are related to the beliefs we have absorbed through experience, family, culture, education ... just from being in the world, and they are often so embedded we are not even aware of their presence. This can sometimes mean that when we think we are viewing things objectively, we are really viewing them through the lens of our assumptions ... so are probably not being objective at all. It's a dilemma, especially when we are often not aware of our bias. But, there is light at the end of this particular tunnel ... by developing our ability to be reflective, we will not only learn where we are making assumptions, we will enhance our ability to think critically and subsequently to change them. The way we think has a significant impact on our behaviours and the quality of our thinking is important, being able to 'think well' is important if we want to make changes. Thinking is of course an automatic process ... things run through our minds in a stream of consciousness, but we can also think more deliberately and thinking involves two distinct processes:

- Automatic thinking which is fast and intuitive – this is the type that requires minimal effort, it might be the decisions we make whilst driving the car or when we briefly notice how someone has responded to something we said.
- Deliberate thinking is much slower and more conscious. This type of thinking requires our focus and a degree of effort. We might use this when we have a big decision to make or when we are trying to resolve a problem.

When we evaluate our practice, we are usually doing so because we want to make some improvements and for this we need a more deliberate approach which involves thinking in a more critical way. Brookfield suggests that there are four aspects to critical thinking, these are:

- Hunting assumptions;
- Checking assumptions;
- Seeing things from different viewpoints;
- Taking action (Brookfield, 2017).

Raising awareness of assumptions is the first step here, but it is important to check their validity – remember what we said about patterns of thinking. Checking assumptions can be done by following a step-by-step process and one technique you could try is the 'down the rabbit hole' (Figure 10.3). This works best if it is an iterative process, so the steps can be repeated several times.

Figure 10.3 Ten-minute reflection – down the rabbit hole

Ten minute reflection – down the rabbit hole

1. Write down your assumption(s) (no editing).
2. Ask why – what is the reason for the assumption(s)?
3. Examine the words ... what are the meanings behind the words? Could these be redefined?
4. Hypothesise – imagine an assumption is removed. What would happen? What if you changed an aspect of it or replaced it with a different assumption?
5. Follow your thoughts down the rabbit hole by repeating each step to uncover further assumptions (Thompson, 2022:47).

There are many things you can do to improve critical thinking. The simple act of regular reflection is a great starting point. In addition, talking through your reflections with a colleague is also helpful. It is amazing how another perspective can give us a whole new outlook. If you would like to try out some practical strategies, the following might be helpful:

Summary rewrite – this strategy is aimed at exploring a narrative in that it considers how we might describe a particular situation and if, in turn, the language we are using is influencing how we feel about it. To do this activity write an account of whatever you want to reflect on, perhaps a dilemma or something that has made you question your views. Go through the account and highlight all of the key words or phrases. Then restate them using different language. This idea is based on the work of Newberg and Waldman (2012) which focusses on the connection between the words we use and our emotions.

Flipping the questions – this has its basis in the idea of questioning assumptions. The starting point is to consider some simple questions such as, 'what information do I have?', 'what might I be overlooking?', 'What do I believe to be true?'. Then you simply flip the questions around:

- What information is missing?
- What do I need to know?
- What do I believe to be false?

Sometimes this activity feels counterintuitive, how can you possibly know what information is missing? But persevere with it, you will be surprised at the new insights you gain.

Storyboarding – This is a useful strategy for those who like to think in images. Take a sheet of A4 or (if you are feeling extravagant) A3 paper and set out a number of boxes as if you were preparing a comic strip. Populate these with images which tell the story of whatever you are reflecting on. You are limited to the space on the page which means that you have to select the key points and need to make decisions about what is important. This is a very powerful strategy for exploring concerns you find difficult to express in words and artistic skills are not required – stick figures will do.

Turning reflection into action

Developing the habit of reflection allows us to think deeply about our practice. This includes the evaluation of single lessons but, if done effectively, goes beyond seeking the quick fix solution. Reflection should help us to see things through different lenses, to find patterns and to explore alternative actions. For those reasons it is something that all teachers should embrace. After all, we don't get better at what we do simply by virtue of experience and being older doesn't necessarily mean being wiser. To improve we have to know what we do well and what could be better, and we then need to think about a number of ways in which we can make the necessary improvements.

Reflection should afford us new insights into our thoughts and actions. We may, as a part of the process, become more self-aware, these are excellent outcomes. But if we reflect, learn and then continue to do things in exactly the same way its usefulness is limited. If we want to make changes then reflection needs to be followed by action, so it is important to consider some strategies which will help this transition.

Change mind map

Reflect on your professional practice and, using your preferred method of mind mapping outline some things you would like to change. Make each of these a branch on your map, then add to each out the branches by including some strategies you would like try.

Mind maps are a form of graphical organiser which allow us to get down a range of thoughts and ideas. They are very fluid in that you can add to them as new things occur to you … you don't need to plan a structure before you start because the format allows you to alter any part of the map. You can also accommodate a lot of information on a single sheet so they are a great way of making sense of your reflections.

Habitual ways of thinking, and being, do provide a sense of security, but they also impose some limits. When we try to generate ideas within the usual *modus operandi* we are automatically limiting our options. One strategy to overcome this is to use the 'no limits' approach in which you write down your ideas in response to the following question: 'If there were absolutely no limits, what would I choose to do?'

It is important that what follows is free thought about what you want to do rather than what you can or should do. Alternatively, you could try writing in a stream of consciousness. Set a timer and write uninterrupted for five minutes, forget about punctuation or any other conventions and just let the ideas flow. This is often used as a strategy in literature to encourage free flowing ideas. It can be equally helpful in reflection.

There are many strategies you can employ to turn your reflection into action, the important thing is that you find your own path. The process is very individual and whilst models and strategies can be a useful kick-start, it is unlikely that any single approach will work for everyone. Whichever way you choose to frame your reflections, if you include the following things, you will most certainly be able to generate new perspectives:

* Notice the detail of events and your actions within them.
* Record what you have noticed and try to include thoughts and feelings.
* Explore things that interest you, read, listen to podcasts, watch clips.
* Think about how the various parts of your reflection might fit together.
* When you want to generate different ideas, be sure to include a range.
* And … remember, reflection is an iterative process, you will revisit topics time and time again and there may not be a single 'magic' solution.

Leveraging learning technology

There are any number of tools and applications that could work for recording and tracking reflections, from something as basic as Microsoft word to a subscription app such as Evernote which will also read the text in images and make them searchable. When thinking about which tools to use for your own reflection consider ease of use above all else. Time is precious and the more barriers there are, the more likely you will lose impetus.

Padlet has already been discussed a number of times throughout this book, all of them focus on how teachers can use the tool with learners, but it can also be incredibly useful for teachers to use themselves. The Padlet app allows you to take live photos of thing like classroom layout or resources/activities that you used and then add notes to them, which will help ensure that you track the important details of your evaluation. We have been using Padlet with trainee teachers for several years and many of them have used the audio feature to record reflections and quick notes. Padlet allows you to choose from a variety of layouts, so you can select something which meets your needs.

Another useful tool for reflection is Trello (https://trello.com/education) which is a workflow and project management tool that allows you to create as many 'lists' as you like on a project board (be sure to use the education link when you sign up). These lists can include things you need to do, are currently doing, things to consider or ideas/reflections. When you want to turn reflection into action, this may well be the tool to choose; items can be colour-coded and you can set due dates for tasks. You can also add links and files to keep things organised. Trello also has a calendar feature to help you keep to deadlines and there are more advanced features that allow you to create your own rules; for example, when you add an item to a 'To Do' list, it automatically creates steps for you to add so you can consider the strategies you need to put in place.

Don't forget that there are several tools built in to your phone that will aid you in your reflective practice. Most smartphones have a voice recorded pre-installed, or a notes app. Post-it notes even have their own app, which will allow you to create an organised digital record of your post-it notes. It may take some experimentation to find the tool that works best for you, but it is worth spending a little time exploring the options.

Summary

In this chapter we have explored the importance of evaluating your practice by developing your skills in critical thinking and reflection. We have discussed why reflection is important in challenging assumptions and have included a range of strategies you could employ. Perhaps the most important point is that reflection should not be limited to single lessons but should become a habit of practice, and to do so we need to find our own path.

References

Brookfield, S. (2017) *Becoming a Critically Reflective Teacher*. San Francisco, CA: John Wiley and Sons.
Davis, W. H. (1911) *'Leisure'*. Available at www.englishverse.com. [Accessed 6 April 23].
Dewey, J. (1910) *How We Think*. Boston, MA: D. C. Heath & Co.
Foucault, M. (1977) *Discipline and Punishment: The Birth of the Prison*. New York, NY: Vintage Books.
Illeris, K. (ed.) (2009) *Contemporary Theories of Learning, Learning Theorists … in Their Own Words*. Oxford: Routledge.
Milne, A. A. (1926) *Winnie the Pooh*. London: Methuen.
Newberg, A. and Waldman, M. R. (2012) *Words Can Change Your Brain*. New York, NY: Plume.
Piaget, J. (1957). *Construction of Reality in the Child*. London: Routledge & Kegan Paul.
Thompson, C. (2022) *Reflective Practice for Professional Development – A Guide for Teachers*. Oxford: Routledge.

11 Individualising learning

Introduction

It is said that Leonardo da Vinci 'confounded' his schoolmaster with insistent questioning, and apparently Einstein was told he 'would never amount to anything'. Even Edison didn't get the best school report; he was considered awkward, and his teacher apparently described him as 'addled' (Gelb and Miller Caldicott, 2009). Aside from somewhat disparaging reports from their teachers, what did these people all have in common? All three were considered to have extraordinary intellectual and creative abilities, in other words they would all be described as genius. This makes us wonder why their teachers didn't see this. We could argue it was a sign of the times, that these are the children of the 'silent generation', the 'seen and not heard' brigade. Perhaps that is true, although they lived in different centuries (Leonardo was around 300 years before the others). Perhaps their teachers were not equipped to spot intellectual or genius tendencies, or maybe they were overly focussed on ensuring that their students were a good fit for the times, learning discipline, manners and skills which would be of use in their future work. Early education for the masses (which didn't really start until the nineteenth century) was certainly focussed on homogeneity – no place for genius there!

We would like to think that modern education establishments are much more enlightened than our Victorian counterparts. After all, we have a vast array of research at our disposal and years of experience on which to base our practice. As part of that enlightenment, we have also recognised that not all learners are the same and if we are to support them to achieve their best, perhaps even help them showcase their genius tendencies, then we need to find a way of personalising teaching and learning. We have already discussed some ideas around this in previous chapters; in Chapter 5, we considered some strategies you can use to adapt learning to meet individual needs, and in Chapter 7 we explored the ways in which teachers can challenge thinking and encourage learner autonomy. In this chapter we are going to take that one step further by discussing how we might use individual goals to shape and build learning.

DOI: 10.4324/9781003385905-12

Individualising learning

If we want to encourage our learners to get the most out of learning, we need to find a way of personalising the experience. As discussed in Chapter 5, we can do this by supporting learners in different ways, but we also need to ensure that personalisation includes challenge, and this is where goals and targets can help learners to flourish.

We are well aware that sometimes setting individual goals can feel like an additional, and perhaps unnecessary task. After all, you have aligned your teaching to the curriculum and have prepared your lessons to meet specific aims – when it comes to supporting learners to achieve, surely you are already doing all the right things? At times, we might be tempted to agree! But there is a caveat. Setting goals and targets can be pointless when its focus is on completing paperwork. That story is very familiar … we are given another document (such as an individual learning plan) that we somehow have to squeeze into an already crowded curriculum and expected to help individual learners come up with meaningful goals and targets. When managed in this way it simply becomes a complicit activity … you know you have to do it, they know you have to do it … no one really wants to, and the result is trite targets that do nothing to inspire further learning. In our experience, when goals and targets are introduced in this way, the paperwork is hurriedly completed, and very often 'individual' goals become homogenous.

Learn from our experience

This excerpt is based on the experience of one of the authors so is written as an individual account.

One moment in my teaching career that I will never forget, occurred right as my learners were about to enter their A2 history exam. The unit was entitled 'Kaiser to Fuhrer' and covered the three governments of Germany from 1900 to 1945. It was a challenging unit and required learners to have an in-depth understanding of what was going on in Germany through both World Wars as well as the impact of the Treaty of Versailles on the German economy during the interwar period. As we were waiting for everyone to turn up, the learners who were already there took the opportunity to look over their notes one last time. One of them caught my attention and said, 'What was the Weimar Republic again?' Now, I always get more nervous than my learners about exams as I tend to panic I have forgotten to teach something which is a key element of the course, so when a student indicated that they didn't know anything about one of the three German governments we had studied, I was flabbergasted and tried to calmly summarise the nature of the Weimar government and its failings, just to try and jog his memory.

As it happens, this particular learner was probably just experiencing some assessment anxiety as he actually did well on the exam, but the experience did make me reflect on my teaching and I wondered how learners could get to the end of a course or even a topic without fully understanding the content. Or maybe having an understanding but not being aware of the scope and limits of that understanding. It hadn't actually occurred to me that as well as checking in with my learners, I needed to challenge them as individuals and make sure that they were able to self-assess their knowledge so that they could seek out, and address, any gaps in it.

This anecdote shows us exactly where the setting of individual goals and targets can have a positive effect, not only in highlighting any gaps in knowledge but also in encouraging learners to take ownership of finding strategies to address those gaps.

The benefits of goals and targets

Despite our somewhat disparaging introduction to the use of goals and targets ... we want to be clear that we genuinely believe that this can be a very productive part of learning and that, rather than being a chore we have to accommodate in our lessons, this can actually be a tool to developing 'expert learners'. Setting clear goals can have a significant impact on both motivation and performance, they provide a direction and focus for learners and show a trajectory of achievement but only if the goals are specific and challenging (Locke and Latham, 2017). 'Tick-box' goals, like the ones mentioned previously, do not present a challenge and when a goal is insufficiently challenging it simply becomes another task. So how do we work with learners to write positive goals, goals which will challenge and inspire them at the same time as being achievable? For starters we need to think about the process and define what we mean by goals and targets, terms which are often used interchangeably.

What are goals and targets?

When we talk about a goal, we are referring to an overall aim. For example, our goal might be to write a book focussed on planning for teaching and learning. We could simply set that as a goal and then go ahead and achieve it, but we might find there is a slight flaw in that plan. Writing anything big like a book or a dissertation is not something you can achieve in an hour or so; it takes a lot of planning and many hours of work. The work also needs to be structured, to include relevant content and to be accessible, so it is unlikely that we would be able to just sit down at the laptop and write, expecting that a few days later we would have the perfect manuscript. To achieve that the work needs to be broken down into several parts and each of those parts needs its own specific aims, and, if you are to achieve the overall goal within a given timeframe, each part also requires a target. So, in a nutshell:

- A goal is an overall aim.
- A target is a specific 'check point' on the way towards a goal – by achieving our targets, we ultimately reach the overall goal.

There are many well-known strategies for setting specific targets and a range of interesting acronyms associated with them, for example SMART – which recommends that we write targets which are specific, measurable, realistic and time constrained. Another popular model is the GROW model (Whitmore, 2009), which is based on the assumption that we need to make some changes. Both work equally well and both are relatively easy to implement, so let's take a look at how they might work in practice.

SMART target setting

This approach is very popular within education circles and we would be surprised if you hadn't heard of it, or even been expected to use it. If you have you will be well aware of the potential benefits and drawbacks. One of the key issues with this model is that specific targets are actually quite difficult to write, and as a result they often end up being written as tasks to complete. A further issue, (probably connected to the first) is that targets set are not sufficiently challenging, and the focus becomes one of completing the paperwork rather than being a meaningful exchange.

Writing SMART targets

Common challenges within your groups are around reading – mainly that learners don't read unless they are specifically requested to do so. You actually want them to read the core text for your subject so that it might inform their learning and get better grades in their assignments, but know that if you ask them to do that, they will approach it in a cursory way, probably just skimming over the selected chapter. Assuming that the overall goal here is to read the core text, try to write one or two targets using the SMART approach.

How easy did you find it to write SMART targets? Was there anything in particular that was difficult? Often, the difficulty arises in being specific, so we might have seen a target along the lines of: 'Read the core textbook by the end of the unit.' That target has a level of specificity, in that it mentions the core text, it may well be realistic, and it is time constrained but is it measurable or specific enough? You might need to take into account the purpose of the goal, which actually goes beyond reading – it is really about reading for a purpose. If you consider that question you could break the target down even further, for example:

- Before the next lesson, select a chapter from the core text which relates to your assignment, and share this with the group.
- Read and make notes from your selected chapter, highlighting three to four key points which are linked to your assignment by ...

These targets are specific, measurable and time constrained. By adding in the additional elements they bring a level of focus that is not present in the first attempt. If you want to take this a step further, you could even convert your goals to the SMARTER format. This has two extra elements which formalise the process a little more, these are:

Specific
Measurable
Achievable

Realistic
Timed
Evaluated
Revised

By adding these two elements, you build in a review which makes the whole process iterative. This is particularly important for target setting as it allows for constructive feedback and refinement so that targets may become even more precise. When working with older learners these additions can be invaluable, but they may well be limiting with a younger age group where the main aim is to introduce goal setting as a useful habit, therefore, you need to think about what will make the process more engaging. Here we would suggest that SMARTER becomes:

Specific
Measurable
Achievable
Timed
Exciting
Rewarding

GROW model

A popular model in business and education, the GROW model is focussed on implementing change (Whitmore, 2009). This is a four-stage model which raises awareness of aspirations and considers possible actions. The basic framework is as follows:

Goal:

What do you want to work on?
What do you want to achieve?

Reality:

How would you rate your current progress?
What do you know already?
What is working well or less well at the moment?

Options:

What could you do differently?
Can you think of some potential options?

Will:

What steps will you take?
When will you complete these steps?

There are similarities to the SMART or SMARTER approach in that the initial focus is on an overall goal, followed by some specific stepping-stones to reaching the goal. In truth, it doesn't really matter which approach you choose. The important thing is how you introduce the idea of individualised learning and how you embed it into your teaching. First and foremost, you need 'buy in'. Your learners need to be made aware of the significant benefits in setting individual goals and they need to know that *you* think it's important. How you introduce the process is crucial to its success, so it is worth giving some thought to that before you implement anything.

Effective goal setting

Preparing for success

How might you introduce the idea of setting goals with your learners? What factors might motivate them? What might put them off? What things need to be in place to enable the process so that it fits seamlessly into your teaching?

You know your learners best so the previous activity should give you something to work with, but it might also be useful to consider what the research suggests about effective goal setting. According to Locke and Latham (1990), if goals are to be motivating then they need to include the three Cs:

- Clarity – the easiest way to achieve this is to select an outcome that is measurable.
- Challenge – goals should have the right amount of challenge – too easy and they won't be motivating, too complex and they become overwhelming.
- Commitment – learners have to be committed to achieving their goals, so they need to be a good fit; this means that they have to be set with a learner and not for them.

It is also helpful if learners receive feedback on their progress towards goals as this provides acknowledgement of what they have done so far and encourages reflection. Of the three Cs listed previously, *challenge* is particularly important as this will have a significant impact on how learners relate to their goals, and it can be quite tricky to get this right. Ultimately, the level of challenge will be established by the task complexity and we need to remember that whilst goals should be challenging, they also need to be achievable. We should also consider how individual learners might respond to pressure. The inverted U model (Figure 11.1) illustrates this effectively, by showing the relationship between pressure and performance – too little pressure and boredom will kick in (remember those 'trite' goals we mentioned earlier?), but too much pressure and we might start to feel anxious that we can't actually achieve what we have set out to do. The middle ground is where we might experience more of a 'flow' state (Csíkszentmihályi, 1990). For this to happen we need a challenge that is interesting and should feel confident we have the skills required to meet

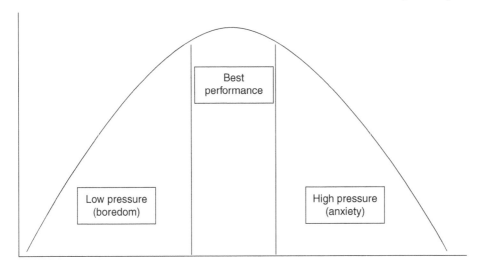

Figure 11.1 Inverted U model

the challenge so that tackling it is not overwhelming. If these conditions are right, we can embrace the challenge and find ourselves totally engaged in the activity.

Pressure factors

As well as considering things which will motivate learners towards setting and achieving their goals, we also need to consider things which could hinder them; what factors will create barriers. There are three things to think about here; we have already discussed the first one, the importance of task complexity, in addition we need to consider skill level and personality:

- Does the learner have (or are they able to acquire) the relevant skills to complete the goal?
- How do they normally respond to pressure?

Taking into account these factors will help to establish appropriate goals which have the right amount of challenge and are motivating to boot!

Positive thinking or positive action

There are a number of benefits to taking a positive outlook and numerous references to back this up (Dweck, 2008; Seligman, 2018). There are a number of benefits to taking a positive outlook and numerous references which suggest that people who are able to think positively, particularly about their ability to manage future events, generally enjoy better health and success (Dweck, 2008; Seligman, 2018). That in itself is inspiring, and we would certainly advocate taking a positive approach rather than a negative one; however, we would also advise against positive thinking which is not attached to positive action. Positive thinking alone will not help you to achieve your goals ... it will most likely provide the inspiration to create some goals and will be a motivational force, but without action it is unlikely to have the desired impact. When working with your learners it is important that they set out their goals when they are motivated and have the necessary drive towards achieving them; however, it is also important that they are prepared for any hurdles that might crop up. To do this, Oettingen (2014) suggests taking a *mental contrasting* approach. This involves imagining future goals, perhaps thinking about what achieving them would look and feel like, then contrasting this with the reality of working towards them. So, we might imagine that we are going to get the prize for 'dissertation of the year', and we then think about what that would mean. The best dissertation would have to be detailed, well written, referenced correctly and so on. We perhaps know that our referencing skills aren't as polished as they could be, and we know we have a tendency to write very long sentences. These are potential hurdles to achieving our overall goal, but they are also things we can overcome if we set targets which are focussed on polishing our skills in these two areas. Not only has this process highlighted potential obstacles, it has made us think about how we can overcome them so that we feel fully prepared and have more confidence in our ability to achieve our goals. A practical strategy which incorporates mental contrasting is the WOOP framework, this includes:

Wish – thinking about what we want to achieve and having a clear sense of what that would look and feel like.
Outcome – creating a specific and measurable goal and thinking about what it would look and feel like to achieve that goal.
Obstacles – this involves imagining the route we need to take from where we are now, to where we need to be and in doing so, considering what obstacles we might encounter. These might take the form of emotions, habits, lack of resources or even the impact of other people.
Plan – now that we have imagined potential difficulties, we can plan how we might overcome them. A helpful strategy here is to employ the if/then technique; if (a particular difficulty) arises, then I will ... by going through potential scenarios we can mentally rehearse overcoming the hurdles which had both a practical and a psychological benefit.

Practical strategies for implementing your goal setting system

As you read this, we suspect you may well be in agreement with the concept of goal setting and recognise the benefits this may have for your learners. We also suspect that, whilst you recognise the benefits, there may be a nagging doubt about how you will be able to implement something else when your time is so stretched. That's a very sensible doubt, indeed it shows that you are applying the WOOPing strategy already! Although we don't have the power to create more time for you, we can make some suggestions which will help you to make the most of what you have. The first is to leverage learning technology (and if you are this far through the book you will already be familiar with that term). The second is to make the goal setting system something which involves others so that the responsibility doesn't entirely fall to you.

Leveraging learning technology

Most schools and colleges will have some sort of Individual Learning Plan tool built into their Learning Information Systems (or Computer Information System, CIS) which will include target setting and review tools. Management information systems such as Promonitor and Compass are examples of this. Most systems allow you set due dates and create calendars for reviewing targets with learners, and in this way, you can make your targets not only SMART but SMARTER.

There are some external tools, focussed on project management, which may help with breaking down and monitoring targets. An excellent example of this is Trello (Trello.com), where users can create to-do lists, targets and tick things off when they have been achieved. Trello could be really useful for reflection, review and target revision. Trello boards can also be shared across teams so they could be used with groups.

Involving others

As discussed in Chapter 5, it is helpful to consider how we work with support staff in order to provide the best experience for learners. As research from the Education Endowment Foundation suggests (EEF, 2015), this isn't something a lot of teachers capitalise on and, as a result, the very important resource we have in the form of an LSA or TA is not used to best effect. However, involvement in individualising learning is something your teaching assistant is very capable of and generally very experienced in. They work closely with learners already so would certainly be able to support them to set realistic and challenging goals in addition to specific targets – you can be involved too, but you don't need to take on the whole responsibility.

Another underutilised classroom resource is the learners themselves. If you have tried peer assessment, you will know that learners can work very effectively together to provide feedback and suggestions for improvements. This is perfect for setting goals and targets, and you may be surprised by how seriously learners take this activity and how much they seem to enjoy it. That said, you may want to set up some initial guidelines to ensure that this is the case.

The expert learner and deliberate practice

We have mentioned the notion of the expert learner in previous chapters and by this we mean learners who take responsibility for their development. Setting goals and specific development targets is a very important part of this and provides individual learners with a framework in which they can make focussed efforts towards achieving the best that they can achieve. But, as we have suggested, simply outlining a goal and writing down some targets isn't going to be enough; they also need to be accompanied by action. They need to be linked to practice.

In Chapter 3 we mentioned the '10,000 hour rule' which is based on the premise that it takes approximately 10,000 hours to become highly skilled at something (Gladwell, 2008). Although, unless you take quite a reductionist approach, strict rules in relation to learning are few and far between, the idea behind this is to emphasise the importance of practice, and it is still helpful to remind ourselves that development takes time. Not only that, it takes deliberate and focussed practice. After all we could spend thousands of hours practising the wrong skills!

This idea is based on the work of Ericsson who recognised that deliberate and focussed practice was more effective in developing expert skills than talent or ability (Ericsson, 2006). So, we don't just practise for a number of hours, we practise in a very deliberate way with specific activities created to improve performance and these activities should include an opportunity to receive feedback. The principles associated with deliberate practice are worth considering when you are thinking about setting individual targets and include:

- Systematic practice – taking into account the order or skill or knowledge acquisition so that development is gradual.
- Practice should be guided – so it is important to build in a review and revise function.
- Motivation is key as some practice may be based on mastery learning and is likely to require repetition in order to improve performance.
- New skills are built onto existing ones, so small changes add up.
- Feedback is required to modify performance and targets.
- Mental representations are helpful in improving performance – using visualisation techniques will help learners to imagine what achieving their goals will look like.

Summary

In this chapter we have highlighted the importance of setting goals and targets to individualise learning and have discussed some strategies which may provide a workable system of goal setting to support learner development. We have also considered a range of strategies for implementing targets which will provide check points en route to achieving overall goals, recommending a system which includes evaluation, review and preparation for potential hurdles.

References

Csíkszentmihályi, M. (1990) *Flow: The Psychology of Optimal Experience*. New York: Harper & Row.

Dweck, C. S. (2008) *Mindset: The New Psychology of Success*. New York: Ballantine.

Education Endowment Foundation (2015) *'Making the Best Use of Teaching Assistants'*. Available at: TA_Guidance_Report_MakingBestUseOfTeachingAssistants-Printable.pdf (educationendowmentfoundation.org.uk) [Accessed 2 June 23].

Ericsson, K. A. (2006) 'The Influence of Experience and Deliberate Practice on the Development of Superior Expert Performance', in K. A. Ericsson, N. Charness, P. J. Feltovich and R. R. Hoffman (eds), *The Cambridge Handbook of Expertise and Expert Performance*. New York: Cambridge University Press, pp. 683–704.

Gelb, M. J. and Miller Caldicott, S. (2009) *Innovate Like Edison: The Five-Step System for Breakthrough Business Success*, New York: Plume.

Gladwell, M. (2008) *Outliers: The Story of Success*. New York: Hachette.

Locke, E. A. and Latham, G. P. (1990) *A Theory of Goal Setting and Task Performance*. Englewood Cliffs, NJ: Prentice Hall.

Locke, E. A. and Latham, G. P. (2017) *New Developments in Goal Setting and Task Performance.* New York: Routledge.

Oettingen, G. (2014) *Rethinking Positive Thinking: Inside the New Science of Motivation.* New York: Penguin Publishing Group.

Seligman, M. (2018) *Learned Optimism: How to Change Your Mind and Your Life.* London: Nicholas Brealey Publishing.

Whitmore, J. (2009) *Coaching for Performance, GROWing Human Potential and Purpose: The Principles and Practice of Coaching an Leadership* (4th edn) London: Nicholas Brealey Publishing.

Final thoughts

Do you remember the script at the beginning of the introduction to this book? Our protagonist silently hoping that they wouldn't be thrown to the lions because they weren't fully prepared for a lesson, whilst inwardly fearing the worst. We hope, after reading this book, that if the same situation occurred, you would be able to approach it with a sense of calm, knowing that you have all the resources you need to, not only to survive such a situation but to thrive on it.

The main aim of this book was to provide practical strategies which would support you in planning great lessons. We also wanted to do that in a way that made use of relevant education theory to ensure that your *great planning* was also informed by *great thinking*. As experienced teachers we all understand the pressure to 'deliver', to ensure that all tasks are complete, and all outcomes are achieved. We are also aware of the need to take a step back occasionally so that we might consider the most effective approaches to support and challenge every learner, as well as creating a motivating environment which encourages learner autonomy and emphasises that the learning journey is a collaborative partnership.

As teachers and learners ourselves, we are all aware of the transformational power of new knowledge and have seen at first hand how a well-planned course, which uses tools to help learners navigate how they are learning as well as encouraging a sense of curiosity, has the power to change someone's life course. We also know that this is only achieved when the course is well planned, not only in the sense of attention to detail but in a way that takes into account all of the factors which affect a classroom. Great planning is genuinely a collaboration between you, your learners and the researchers who provide a little food for thought, and we now hope that we too are a part of that collaboration.

It has been a pleasure sharing our thoughts and experience with you!

Carol, Lydia, Elaine, Ann and Mark

DOI: 10.4324/9781003385905-13

APPENDIX
The ILT A-Z

Welcome to the ILT A-Z list. Many of the tools and websites mentioned here are explored in the chapters of the book where we review the use of applications in relation to theory and practice; however, there are a lot of tools out there and we knew we could never cover them all. We thought it would be useful, particularly for new teachers or teachers looking to develop their practice, to have a handy list of tools to explore. This is that list, although there are surely still things that did not make the list or simply ones we haven't yet heard of. We will use the Padlet page as a tool to update this appendix from time to time. Most of the tools here are free or the discussion focuses on the free side of the tool, but there are a few paid tools that we felt still deserved to be here. For now we hope you find this useful as a guide.

App/website	Brief description	Pros/cons	Chapters
A			
AudacityTeam.org	Simple but powerful audio recording/ editing suite for podcasting.	Pros: Open-source, so free forever; lots of powerful tools; easy to add multiple tracks; runs on any PC or Mac Cons: Most tools you won't use but can feel intimidating so find a basic intro tutorial on YouTube.com	Chapter 7

(Continued)

App/website	Brief description	Pros/cons	Chapters
B			
Blooket.com	This is a web tool, which allows teachers to create or access banks of questions and then set up a range of games for learners to play using those questions.	Pros: Easy to use, lots of questions available already, engaging for learners, free (there is a paid side with additional features). Cons: Learners need access to an individual device	Chapter 3 Chapter 4
Blendspace.com	An online flipped learning tool that allows you to easily take content you already have and build an online lesson from it.	Pros: Free, incredibly easy to use, just add your presentations, documents/ worksheets, and videos in the order you want them to be seen by students and add an assessment at the end. Cons: You can make lessons private, but the terms of service mean that your content (presentations, etc.) can be made public and shared with other teachers.-	
C			
Canva.com/ education	Design and template website which allows learners to create brilliant presentations, posters and other documents without having to have graphic design skills.	Pros: Free for life if you get the education account. Thousands of designs available. Teachers can create classes and assignments. Any document can be turned into a website. New features are being added all the time. Cons: Not many - can be a bit overwhelming to find a design as there are a number to choose from.	
ChatGPT	An artificial intelligence chat tool that can engage in realistic and informed conversations and answer questions.	Pros: The best way to consider pros is to ask ChatGPT itself, the response is pretty extensive and includes some of the cons to consider as well. Writes a pretty good lesson plan as a starting point for teachers (although you will, of course, have to adapt it). Cons: ChatGPT has been getting a lot of bad press in education around issues with plagiarism, which is a concern, but can be addressed through creative assessment (e.g. Chat GPT can't produce a video essay) and knowing your learners' ability.	Chapter 8

App/website	Brief description	Pros/cons	Chapters
Classtools.net	A collection of teacher tools including graphic organisers, Facebook chat generators, game builders and even a QR treasure hunt builder.	Pros: Completely free, lots of tools/ games to choose from, can build classic video games with any bank of 10 questions. Cons: Some elements look quite dated, video game generators require you to type the questions in a very specific way in order to work.	
Clickview.com	An educational video platform that allows you to capture, edit and share content that airs on live TV and a virtually endless bank of other content.	Pro: Really easy to use and really powerful. Allows teachers to edit, clip and share videos with learners through Virtual Learning Environments (VLEs). Cons: Big issue is that although there is a free trial, it is a paid tool.	
Colorveil – App	Colourveil is an app you can download on a PC or onto a memory stick to run as a portable app, which allows you to put a colour overlay on top of anything on the screen.	Pros: Its free. Really simple to use and change the colour and the transparency of the 'veil'. The option to run it as a portable app means learners can just have it on a memory stick and use it on any computer, which is amazing flexibility. Teachers can simply adjust the colour overlay on any presentation. Cons: as it has to be installed or run portable, you may need permissions from your IT team to install it if you can't use a memory stick.	Chapter 5
Crash Course	A great YouTube channel which has educational content on a range of subjects.	Pros: Tons of great content across a broad range of subjects. Extensive depth and explanations of concepts. Engaging videos with great animations and a sense of humour. Cons: Some students may find them a bit too fast paced, but they can always rewatch.	
D Dragon speech to text	This is probably the leading speech to text app on the market and just keeps getting better at creating a fluid user experience for writers to create documents.	Pros: For learners who have used this tool, it has been nothing short of a game changer, helping them fluidly create content for assessments without the blank page being a barrier. For HE, student finance may support the cost for learners with identified needs. Cons: This is a paid subscription and can be rather costly.	

(Continued)

App/website	Brief description	Pros/cons	Chapters
E			
Eventbrite	An event management and ticketing website that lets you easily keep track of how many are attending an event, who they are and even issues electronic tickets.	Pros: It is straightforward to use and easy to sign up. It is free for any free event, you only get charged for events that you charge for. Has analytics and reporting and can easily tie into social media tools. Cons: None that we can think of if you are hosting an event, it's great and the free to use for free events is perfect for educational applications.	
edpuzzle.com	An online tool for teachers to create online video lessons.	Pros: Free for up to 20 videos so you really get to have a go before you even think about paying for anything. You can add assessments to any video. There are a large number of of videos already there for you to use. Cons: TedEd (see below) is pretty similar and totally free.	
F			
Flipgrid.com	A website and associated app that allows teachers to pose questions to learners and get video/audio responses.	Pros: A great formative assessment method, really valid assessment, learners can vote and like each other's posts, teachers have total control over comments etc., built into Microsoft Teams. Cons: Will take a few tries for learners to get used to it and get comfortable with recording their responses (try the first few times in class).	Chapter 9
Filmora	Filmora is a video editing software with associate apps that allow you to stitch images and video clips and overlay music.	Pros: A great tool that is pretty straight forward and powerful. allows you to create multiple layers. Free to use as long as you don't mind a watermark on the final video. Cons: Subscription costs are either monthly or you can pay for lifetime access.. Sometimes too many options can put new users off.	Chapter 7
Facebook.com	A social media app, that most likely you have already heard of.	Pros: Consider how you might leverage social media apps to share what you do in class. To have learners create content they can share and post, work they can be proud of is very powerful. Cons: Obviously there are lots of data and safeguarding issues to be aware and cautious of.	

App/website	Brief description	Pros/cons	Chapters
G			
Gapminder.org	This is a website dedicated to helping people modify their understanding of the world, based on real data not the influence of media. There are a ton of good resources here especially the quiz and gapminder world which allows you to adjust and manipulate data in really engaging ways.	Pros: Totally free. Based on reputable UN data, perfect for history, sociology and science classes especially. Good resources available for teachers. Cons: Can take a bit of playing with to get your head around it.	Chapter 8
Google forms	Built in element of any Google email or education account (part of Google Drive), which allows you to build simple and complex surveys for feedback, research and even quizzes.	Pros: Relatively easy to use with loads of question types; responses can be set to automatically be entered in a spread sheet; Quiz can self-mark and even email results to learners; teachers can add their own feedback to responses. Cons: Can take some getting used to when wanting to build more advanced questionnaires with conditional questions.	Chapter 9
H			
Hotpotatoes	A suite of six applications that let you create interactive multiple-choice, short-answer questions and more. https://hotpot.uvic.ca/	Pros: Easy to use and completely free. Lots of question types. Cons: Requires installation so may need IT approval. Hot Potatoes has been around a while and although it is still really good it looks its age.	
I			
Instagram	A social media app which could be a great way to promote learner work and communicate success with families.	Pros: Easy to use, access and share. Trainees who have done action research on this have found that learners really engage in creating work to be posted and that increases engagement of potential students. Cons: As with Facebook, tread carefully in relation to GDPR and Safeguarding.	

(Continued)

App/website	Brief description	Pros/cons	Chapters
Immersive Reader	A Microsoft tool that will read any document out loud for learners.	Pros: Easy to use, built into Office 365. Great accessibility tool, will read any selected text in Edge as well. Speed can be adjusted so learners can use it at their own pace. Cons: None really, a great accessibility tool.	Chapter 5
J			
Jeopardylabs.com	Jeopardy is an American quiz show in which contestants are given the answer and need to come up with the question, which always begins with 'What is …'	Pros: Loads of pre-built quizzes, you can embed videos and audio files, create templates and control the privacy. Cons: There is a cost, but it is relatively inexpensive for a lifetime subscription.	
K			
Kahoot.it	An engaging quiz website and app that creates healthy competition between learners.	Pros: Really easy to use, tons of pre-built questions sets, ghost mode allows for learners to play against their previous score. Cons: Free side has become quite limited, questions appear on screen and the answers on learner devices (screen switching is a challenge for some learners).	Chapter 4
Kialo.com	A debating tool for teachers and students that tracks the pros and cons of an issue.	Pros: Powerful tool which is great for higher order thinking. Can control comments and students can vote on responses. Teachers can require students to provide evidence. Cons: It can take a moment to get your head around, but the payoff is well worth it.	Chapter 3 Chapter 6 Chapter 7
L			
Linkedin	A professional social media tool that can help your learners build a professional identity.	Pros: A great way to get learners thinking about next steps. A good tool for tracking progression and next steps of learners. Cons: As with all social media, be aware of safeguarding issues.	
M			
Mentimeter	An online presentation and assessment tool that allows you to build really interactive presentations, polls and assessments	Pros: Fairly simple to use; a good range of tools (word cloud tool is great). Cons: Free side is limited to how many activities can be used in a presentation.	

App/website	Brief description	Pros/cons	Chapters
Microsoft Forms	Microsoft's version of Google forms, allows you to easily create surveys, polls and quizzes.	Pros: Simple to use and really easy to share with learners (especially if you are in a Microsoft institution). Cons: Not Google forms (the graphs and power of Google's version is just a bit better).	
Miro.com	Online digital whiteboard which allows you to create, share and even invite users to contribute to notes or presentation.	Pros: Go to https://miro.com/cont act/education/?ref=Educator to get a free teacher account, lots of templates to create mind maps, great tool for sharing and collecting ideas from a group. Cons: Would be great if there was a feature to turn a mind map into a presentation.	Chapter 3
N			
Nearpod	An all-in-one presentation and assessment website with associated app. Allows teachers to deliver content directly to learners' phones/devices for effective and engaging delivery.	Pros: A popular choice for online delivery, a great range of assessment and activity tools (fill in the blanks, matching, drawing are just some examples), easy to use and to embed multimedia, can upload existing PowerPoint slides. Cons: Free side has limited storage, presentation slides are pretty basic PowerPoint style.	Chapter 5
O			
Onenote.com	A Microsoft tool that allows users to keep track of and share notes, documents etc. Class notebook is the education and teacher version.	Pros: A powerful classroom management tool that can be leveraged to set, share and monitor work with learners. Great for collaboration. Cons: As it is part of the Microsoft Suite your school will need to be a Microsoft school to have full access to class notebook.	
Openoffice.com	A free version of office tools including word processing, presentation and spreadsheet tools.	Pros: As many office tools have attached costs, access to powerful free tools closes the digital divide. This gives all students access to these tools on any computer they have at home. Cons: It's a free and powerful tool – what problems can there be? Well just the one that sometimes the filetype can be fiddly in other office tools, but it is easily fixed.	

(Continued)

App/website	Brief description	Pros/cons	Chapters
P			
Padlet.com	An online bulletin/ notice board where you can easily post all sorts of content to share with learners, get learners to contribute to or get them to create their own and build portfolios. Use cases are nearly endless.	Pros: Hands down the tool we use more than any other, easy to use and you can even add audio and video to your pages, has built-in approval settings so you can authorise any post, profanity filter, built-in QR code generator makes it really easy to share, easy to archive old Padlets you aren't using, we could go on and on ☺. Cons: Limited to 3 active Padlets on free account (you can get more by sharing a sign-up link from your account, every 3 people that use it gets you an extra page).	Chapter 5 Chapter 6 Chapter 7 Chapter 8
Plickers	An assessment tool where the teacher is the only one who needs a device.	Pros: Free account is really good (limited reporting), only the teacher needs a device (for scanning learner responses), learners only need a QR code you print from the website, easy to create groups and classes and assign questions, teachers can control the live screen from their phones and choose questions to ask, group size up to 64, really accessible for learners, easy for the teacher to scan responses fast, learners can change their answers. Cons: Has a shorter shelf life than Kahoot or Quizizz (learners will get bored after about 5 questions), if a learner puts their fingers over the code your phone won't read it.	
Poll Everywhere	The original online assessment tool- allows learners to SMS/text message their responses straight in (no internet needed)	Pros: Fairly easy to use and you can create banks of questions in sets of 5, if you have unreliable internet this is a good option, can be embedded straight into PowerPoint. Cons: A bit more fiddly than app-based options as you need to begin your answer with a code.	
Prezi	A presentation tool with a difference. Lots of templates for designing unique looking presentations.	Pros: A great change from PowerPoint, more like teaching from a mind map, free for teachers (first level of paid account anyway). Cons: The original was arguably better, does take a little getting used to create one.	

App/website	Brief description	Pros/cons	Chapters
Q			
QRstuff.com	A QR code creator/ generator website.	Pros: free to use for the basic QR codes, easy to use, also has a built-in reader which works on any device. Cons: Have to do one code at a time and download It, has ads unless you pay.	
Quizbusters	A free plenary quiz tool that allows teachers to create class teams that compete against one another.	Pros: Completely free. Lots of pre-built quizzes. Supports foreign languages. Cons: A bit dated, but some old stuff still works well.	
Quizizz.com	A web-based assessment/quiz tool with lots of prebuilt quizzes and a lot of question types. Has a companion app for learners to access quizzes.	Pros: This is simply the best of these types of sites out there. Broad range of questions to get at higher order thinking, great reports at the end of the quiz for tracking that can inform teaching. Easy to use and allows teachers to shuffle questions and answers for greater reliability. Cons: Some really good features are now behind a paywall. The music will haunt your dreams.	Chapter 4 Chapter 6
Quizlet.com	Allows teachers to create a great range of online assessments for learners as well as flash cards etc.	Pros: Really easy to use to create engaging content to share with learners. Cons: Only free for 30 days then an annual subscription is required.	
R			
Renderforest.com	Online video and animation tool.	Pros: Easy to use and lots of stock elements that you can use. A range of pre-built templates, scenes etc. Cons: Free account is limited in access to stock images and storage. Paid version is a monthly subscription.	
S			
Screencastomatic. com	Screen recording tool allows you to easily turn whatever you are doing on your computer into a video.	Pros: Really easy to use; no need to install any software; Education pricing is reasonable. Cons: Limited to 15 minutes on free account.	Chapter 7

(Continued)

App/website	Brief description	Pros/cons	Chapters
Slideshare.net	A platform for teachers and creators to share presentations and other documents.	Pros: A great way for teachers (especially new teachers) to avoid having to reinvent the wheel and access good materials to start from. Saves a ton of time when teaching or planning for new content. Cons: Be sure to check materials thoroughly before you use them, people make mistakes and/or teach differently from the way you do.	
Socrative.com	A quiz tool, which allows learners to join quiz sessions and complete a prepared set of questions.	Pros: Has a team race mode which can randomly assign learners to a team for competition – reduces individual pressure; exit ticket can be done on the go; allows for open questions. Cons: Not as flashy as Quizizz/Kahoot so learners get bored faster.	Chapter 6
Sporcle.com	Online quiz website with millions of prebuilt quizzes on just about anything you can think of.	Pros: Really easy to access; incredible range of quizzes and topics; completely free unless you want to remove adds; all users can make quizzes. Cons: Ads can be a little annoying; user created quizzes give you variety, but that means some are better than others.	Chapter 3 Chapter 8
Sutori.com	A presentation tool which builds presentations like a timeline.	Pros: Really clean and simple design; easy to use and add media. Cons: Free side is somewhat limited; a bit pricey on the paid side.	
Sway.office.com	A Microsoft presentation tool that works a bit like a scrolling billboard.	Pros: Part of Office 365; a nice change from PowerPoint; can be used in a number of ways, even as a newsletter or collection of materials for learners to explore. Cons: Takes a bit of getting used to.	
T			
Teachertube.com	YouTube for teachers.	Pros: Lots of great educational content, organised by subject, much of it created by other teachers. content is built for education. Cons: It isn't quite YouTube – there will always be less content than on the main channel.	

App/website	Brief description	Pros/cons	Chapters
Ted.com	'Ideas worth spreading' A collection of riveting and engaging talks from prominent figures in fields of technology, entertainment, design and many others.	Pros: Completely free, open access; great source of inspiration for learners. Can be used with TEDEd to create a lesson. Cons: Addicting to watch and easy to go down a rabbit hole.	Chapter 8
TEDEd (ed.ted. com)	A tool that allows you to create a lesson out of any video on TED.com, ed.ted. com or YouTube. com.	Pros: Completely free; you can flip any lesson and make it your own, range of assessment options (open and closed questions, extension tasks, discussion forum); best flipped learning tool on the web. Cons: Learners need to create an account if you want to be able to track their completion of work.	Chapter 8
Thingiverse.com	A nearly endless collection of designs for 3D printers and laser cutter.	Pros: An open source collection of thousands of designs and models for anything you might want to print on a 3D printer. Cons: The site is becoming a little dated. Other sites like Thangs.com and Printables are also really good.	
Thinglink.com	The expression goes that a picture is worth a 1,000 words, Thinglink makes that literal as you can add text, video and links to any image.	Pros: Great tool for creating interactive infographics/images, paid side can even work for good VR content, fairly easy to use. Cons: Free side is good but a little limited.	
Tricider.com	A social voting tool allows teachers to collect ideas and then have learners vote on them.	Pros: Really straightforward to use, great way to drive group decision making or vote on debates. Cons: Somewhat limited use cases as it is quite specialised but good at what its designed for.	
U Ultimaker cura	A 3D printing slicer that is free and open source. A slicer turns any 3D design file (.stl file) into layers so it can be printed on a 3D printer.	Pros: The industry leading slicer, which can work with virtually any printer on the market. Cons: Does require an install – so may need IT support/permission.	

(Continued)

App/website	Brief description	Pros/cons	Chapters
V			
Visme.co	A tool for creating presentations, videos and infographics.	Pros: Free to sign up and try. Lots of templates to use as a starting point. Cons: Free side is limited to 100 MB.	
Vocaro.com	A voice recording and voice note sharing app.	Pros: Easily share and send voice notes via email to anyone you like. Notes can be easily deleted or deleted automatically after a few months. Doesn't require login or user profiles. Cons: Does have Google adds – that is how it is free.	
W			
Wakelet.com	A UK-based Padletesque tool. Allows you to post a range of content on a notice board style.	Pros: Easy to use, has some similar features to Padlet. Cons: It's not Padlet.	Chapter 5 Chapter 8
Wetransfer.com	A great tool for transferring large files via email.	Pros: Easy to upload large files and email a download link to anyone. A great way for art learners to share work, videos, you name it. Free for files up to 2 GB. Files delete automatically after 7 days. You don't need an account to start using it. Cons: Not a good way to send sensitive or personal information or documents.	
X			
Xml notepad	A straightforward tool for editing or creating Xml documents/files. Xml is a data transfer and display language. Like HTML it tells your computer how to arrange text and images on a computer screen.	Pros: Free tool which is useful for anyone doing digital design. Cons: It is getting a bit dated, but not hard to make an argument for its continued relevance.	
Y			
YouTube.com	Unless you have been living under a rock you likely know this is the world's largest video hosting website.	Pros: Endless content for teachers to use, free account comes with any Google account, easy to search and find content, a bit more effort to create your own. Cons: Ads, ads and more ads, Be sure to preview content before you use it.	

App/website	Brief description	Pros/cons	Chapters
Z			
Zoom.com	An online meeting platform used for hosting lessons, and meetings.	Pros: Easy to use and one of the market leaders in this technology. Lots of built in tools for teachers to use and apps that can be added. Free to sign up. Cons: There Is a fee for hIgher level usage. Google meet and Microsoft Teams are very similar and may already be part of your school infrastructure.	
Zotero.org	A referencing tool that you can add right into Google Chrome.	Pros: Easy to use and a powerful tool for organising sources. Can take snapshots of websites. Builds right into Google docs. Cons: There are always small differences in referencing style so when you use it for references you may still need to check it over.	

INDEX